Marriages
of
Middlesex County Virginia

- 1740-1852 -

Compiled by:
The Virginia Genealogical Society

Southern Historical Press, Inc.
Greenville, South Carolina

SOUTHERN HISTORICAL PRESS, INC.
PO BOX 1267
Greenville, SC   29601

ISBN #0-89308-265-1

Printed in the United States of America

PREFACE

Here is another valuable addition to the ever-growing interest in genealogy and the American past, particularly the early history of the tidewater counties of Virginia.

A group of capable and informed genealogists, all members of the Virginia Genealogical Society, have undertaken, as a project of the Society, the publication of the marriage bonds of Middlesex County for the years 1740 through 1852. These ladies are Mesdames Phyllis Wright, Isobel Woodson, Joyce Lindsay, Virginia Livingston, Emma R. Matheny and Helen K. Yates. They may be seen day after day in the Archives Division in diligent pursuit of genealogical information and historical facts. Well qualified in the field, there can be no doubt that this publication contains as near a perfect transcription as it is possible for them to obtain.

Middlesex County was formed in the year 1673 from Lancaster County on the other side of the Rappahannock River in what is called the Northern Neck of Virginia. The County was the seat in Virginia's Golden Age of some of the fairest names of the old order. The Churchills of Wilton, the Wormeleys of Rosegill, the Grymes of Brandon, the Robinsons of Hewick, the Gordons, the Armisteads, the Lees and many others. Here was the home of the distinguished Arthur Lee.

These marriage bonds and ministers returns are, of course, not complete. For the years 1768, 1769, 1770, 1771 and 1841 there are no marriage records. The earliest marriages are not included in this work as they may be found in the Christ Church Parish Register. Of course, there will likely be duplication of some marriages recorded in both the Parish Register and the marriage records of the County.

From personal observation, I feel that this work will be a most reliable and valuable contribution to the Archives of Virginia, and the Society is to be commended for its efforts.

Richmond, Virginia
January 26, 1965

Edward Chase Earle Jr.

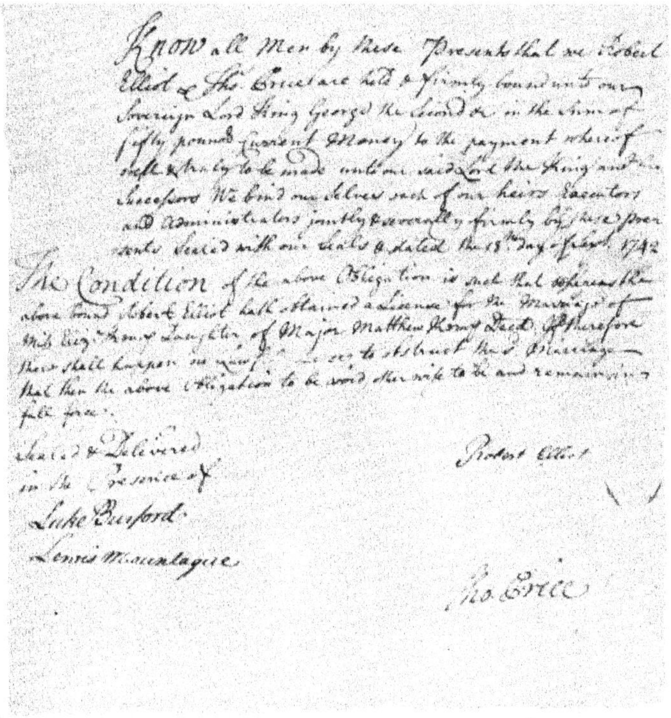

Know all Men by these Presents that we Robert Elliot & Tho. Price are held & firmly bound unto our Sovereign Lord King George the Second &c in the Sum of fifty pounds Current Money to the payment whereof well & truly to be made unto our said Lord the King and his Successors We bind our selves each of our heirs Executors and Administrators jointly & severally firmly by these presents Sealed with our Seals & dated the 18th Day of Sept. 1742

The Condition of the above Obligation is such that whereas the above bound Robert Elliot hath obtained a Licence for the Marriage of Miss Eliz. Kemp Daughter of Major Matthew Kemp Dec'd. If therefore there shall happen no lawful cause to obstruct the sd Marriage that then the above Obligation to be void else to be and remain in full force.

Sealed & Delivered in the Presence of

Luke Burford

Lewis Mountague

Robert Elliot

Tho. Price

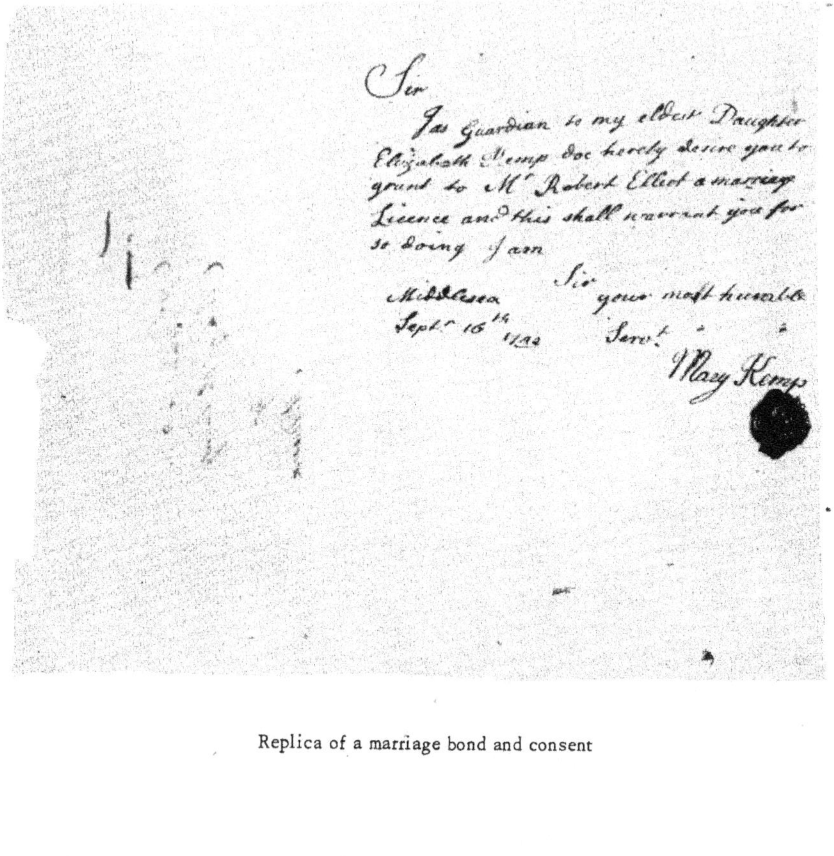

Sir

I as Guardian to my eldest Daughter Elizabeth Kemp doe hereby desire you to grant to Mr Robert Elliot a marriage Licence and this shall warrant you for so doing I am

Middlesex Septr 16th 1742

Sir your most humble Servt

Mary Kemp

Replica of a marriage bond and consent

ABBOTT, Bivvin and Nancy Dejarnett. Bond 15 June 1801. Nancy is above
21 years and is the daughter of Daniel Dejarnett, deceased. Married
18 June 1801 by Henry Heffernan. Sur. and Wit. Thomas Ferguson. p.53.

ABRAMS, Absalom A. and Elizabeth Watts. Bond 1 May 1804. Elizabeth is
above 21 years. Sur. and Wit. Staige Davis, Thomas D. Watts, and
Samuel Wood. p. 58.

AILWORTH, Edmund and Sarah E. Anderton. Bond 31 December 1845. James
S. Bristow guardian of Sarah. Married 31 December 1845 by George
Northam. Sur. and Wit. John P. Bristow. p. 130.

AILWORTH, Josiah and Miss Roberta Seward. Bond 24 December 1832. Sur.
and Wit. Nathan Healy. p.110.

AILWORTH, Lenox and Mildred Dudley. Bond 5 February 1829. Married
7 February 1829 by George Northam. Sur. and Wit. William Ailworth,
Malvina Dudley, and Milhage (?) Dudley who consents. p.100.

ALDERSON, Reuben and Mary Taff. Bond 16 February 1781. Sur. and Wit.
Jacob Stiff Saunders. p.24.

ALDIN, John and Elizabeth Lee. Bond 7 December 1762. George Lee, deceased, father of Elizabeth. Sur. and Wit. William Meacham, who gives
consent, John Lewis, and James Wortham. p.14.

ALDRIDGE, Adam and Catharine Jackson. Bond 7 March 1783. Sur. and Wit.
John Jackson, Jr. p.27.

ALLCOCK, Robert, bachelor, and Miss Mary Alliot, spinster. Bond 1 July
1760. Sur. and Wit. John Murray and Phil Mountague. p.12.

ALLEN, William of New Kent County, under age, and Miss Clara Walker. Bond
7 December 1753. James Baker, of Isle of Wight County, guardian of
William. Christopher Robinson, William Taliaferro, give consent for
Clara. Sur. and Wit. Henry Thacker, Richard Townes, Richard Baker,
Daniel Fisher, Jr., Sarah Robinson, Robert Armistead, and Lewis
Willis. p.8.

ALMORE, Capt. Samuel and Rachel McKan. Bond 21 April 1792. Sur. and
Wit. William Hoskins, Benjamin Churchill, and John McKan. p.38.

ANDERSON, Alexander and Nancy Scott. Bond 25 November 1780. Sur. and
Wit. Delphos Scott. p.24.

ANDERTON, John and Mrs. Elizabeth Layton, widow of Richard Laton, deceased. Bond 5 September 1816. Elizabeth signed own consent. Sur. and Wit. William Barker. p.81.

ANDERTON, John G. and Miss Elizabeth D. Bristow, daughter of Benjamin Bristow. Bond 16 February 1816. Sur. and Wit. Benjamin Bristow. p.80.

ANDERTON, William and Miss Elizabeth Pritchet. Bond 3 June 1824. Sur. and Wit. George Dudley. p.89.

ARMISTEAD, John and Mary Churchhill, daughter of Armistead Churchhill, Esquire. Bond 23 November 1749. Sur. and Wit. William Churchhill, and William McDuff. p.5.

ARMSTRONG, William H. and Martha A. Garrett. Bond 13 October 1847. Married 13 October 1847 by R. A. Christian. Sur. and Wit. Robert H. Bray and Agnes Garrett. p.132.

ASSELIN, David of Gloucester County and Elizabeth Stubblefield. Bond 19 October 1750. Sur. and Wit. Thomas Laughlin. p.5.

ATKINS, John and Ann Burton. Bond 23 August 1773. Sur. and Wit. Thomas Burton. p.18.

ATKINSON, Almond and Miss Mary D. Rose, daughter of Thomas Rose. Bond 8 March 1834. Sur. and Wit. James Jones. p.113.

ATKINSON, George and Catharine Knowles. Bond 15 June 1795. Married 18 June 1795 by Robert Ware. Sur. and Wit. John B. Garland. p.42.

BADLEY, Peter Joshua and Anne Anderson Batchelder. Bond 20 December 1788. Married 23 December 1788 by Samuel Klug. Sur. and Wit. Anderson Miller [also shown as Andeson Miler] and Christopher Robinson. p.33.

BAKER, James and Johnna Bray. Bond 29 April 1788. Married 3 May 1788 by Samuel Klug, who gives the name as Susanna Bray. Sur. and Wit. Thomas Patterson and Will. Churchhill. p.32.

BALL, Austin and Sarah Jackson. Bond 12 August 1812. John Jackson, deceased, father of Sarah. Catharine Stamper is her guardian. Sur. and Wit. Vincent W. Faucett and Elizabeth Young. p.75.

BALL, Joseph and Mrs. Frances Wyatt. Bond 3 December 1844. Married in December 1844 by Thomas B. Evans [the day omitted from the minister's return] Sur. and Wit. William P. Woodward. p.126.

BALL, Williamson of Richmond County, and Priscilla Span, widow. Bond 9 February 1765. Sur. and Wit. Will. Churchhill. p.16.

BANKS, Tunstall and Polly Murray Curtis. Bond 22 May 1793. Charles Curtis, guardian of Polly. Sur. and Wit. William Roane. p.40.

BARBEE, George and Martha Fagan, widow. Bond 22 June 1759. Sur. and
Wit. James Davis and John Chowning. p.11.

BARNETT, Joseph and Felisha George. Bond 2 March 1843. Married 2 March
1843 by Richard A. Christian. Sur. and Wit. Thomas Mason, Thomas J.P.
Mason, and Custis Wessets. p.122.

BARRICK, Baylor and Sally S. Saunders. Bond 16 March 1803. Sur. and
Wit. Benjamin Bristow. p.56.

BARRICK, David and Mrs. Mary Layton, of age. Bond 29 December 1807. Married 29 December 1807 by David Corey. Sur. and Wit. Bailey Barrick,
Samuel Blake. p.65.

BARRICK, David and Miss Sarah Long, daughter of Robert Long. Bond 4 January 1820. Wit. Robert Long. p.84.

BARRICK, John B. and Elizabeth Layton. Bond 7 December 180 . Married
7 December 1808 by David Corey. Sur. and Wit. George Layton and
Joseph Boss. p.65.

BARRICK, George W. and Miss Nancy Blake. Bond 8 April 1843. Sur. and Wit.
James Mercer and William J. Barrick. p.123.

BARRICK, Henry D. and Miss Virginia A. Pace. Bond 14 August 1844. George
D. Pace, guardian of Virginia. Married 15 August 1844 by George
Northam. Sur. and Wit. Andrew Stiff. p.126.

BARRICK, John M. and Miss Emeline Duncan. Bond 27 December 1830. Married
27 December 1830 by George Northam. Sur. and Wit. Henry Northam. p.105.

BARRICK, Robert and Lucinda L. Jackson, widow. Bond 20 April 1801. Married
23 April 1801 by Henry Heffernan. Sur. and Wit. Peter Robinson and
George Pace. p.52.

BARRICK, Robert and Elizabeth Wood Healy. Bond 2 March 1808. Sur. and
Wit. John C. Warwick. p.66.

BARRICK, Robert and Miss Sarah C. Lee, daughter of Charles Lee, deceased.
Bond 13 May 1813. Sur. and Wit. William Oldham and Churchill Blakey.
p.76.

BARRICK, William and Judith Palmer, of lawful age. Bond 20 January 1808.
Married 18 January 1808 by David Corey. Sur. and Wit. Robert Barrick.
p.66.

BARRICK, William F. and Nora Long. Bond 22 May 1848. Married 31 May 1848·
by Holland Walker. Sur. and Wit. Robert Blake. p.134.

BARROCK, David D. and Miss Matilda Oliver. Bond 8 May 1844. Sur. and Wit.
Ythel M. Parry and Thomas Wood. p.125.

BARROCK, David D. and Miss Jane Didlake. Bond 11 March 1845. Sur. and Wit. William H. Haile and Richard D. Stoner. p.128.

BARROCK, John and Frances Wood. Bond 29 October 1799. Sur. and Wit. William B. Hodges and Josiah Burns. p.50.

BARTLET, Benjamin and Lavinia Bird, of age. Bond 14 March 1807. Mary Vowel, mother of Lavinia and also her guardian. Sur. and Wit. Thomas Clarke and Thomas Montague, Jr. p.64.

BATCHELDER, Henry and Elizabeth Dillard. Bond 29 March 1785. Sur. and Wit. Thomas Healy. p.28.

BATCHELDER, James and Mary Jackson. Bond 13 March 1792. Sur. and Wit. William Jackson and W. Segar. p.38.

BATCHELDER, John and Elizabeth Mickelburrough. Bond 15 February 1748. Henry Mickelburrough, father of Elizabeth. Sur. and Wit. Henry Mickelburrough and Richard Major. p.4.

BATCHELDER, Samuel and Elizabeth Laughlin. Bond 2 May 1747. Thomas Laughlin, father of Elizabeth. Sur. and Wit. Richard Major. p.4.

BATCHELDOR, John and Ruth Smith. Bond 4 March 1744. John Smith, father of Ruth. Sur. and Wit. John Smith. p.2.

BAYTEN (BADEN), William and Sarah Rhodes. Bond 24 December 1773. Sur. and Wit. Benjamin Rhodes and Edmond Cowles. p.19.

BAYTOP, James and [Catherine B. Yates.] Bond 31 December 1807. Married 31 December 1807 by Henry Heffernan. Sur. and Wit. Anthony New. [The name of the wife was omitted from the marriage bond, but was shown on the minister's return.] p.65.

BEAMAN, John and Rebecca Row. Bond 28 September 1786. Married 1 October 1786 by William Mullins. Sur. and Wit. John Clarke. p.30.

BEDDOO, Zedekiah and Lucy F. Wiatt. Bond 10 May 1830. Major Wiatt, deceased, father of Lucy. Rawleigh Rains and Susan Rains, her guardians. Sur. and Wit. Joseph Clarkson and John Hardy. p.103.

BEAMON, Lynes and Jane Montague. Bond 23 July 1810. Lewis Montague, deceased, father of Jane. William Parron gives consent. Sur. and Wit. John Clark, George Healy, and Henry Muse. p.70.

BENNETT, Smith and Miss Sally Webbmore (Webmore), of age. Bond 9 December 1812. Sur. and Wit. Edmund Healy. p.76.

BENNETT, William J. and Adeline Miller. Bond 1 January 1845. Married 1 January 1845 by George Northam. Sur. and Wit. Robert Blake. p.127.

BERRY, James A. and Mrs. Mary Ann Bennett. Married 27 January 1842 by Lewis H. Williams. [Minister's return only.] p. 164.

BERRY, John and Elizabeth Robinson. Bond 28 December 1785. Married
31 December 1785 by Samuel Klug. Sur. and Wit. Charles Blake. p.29.

BERRY, John D. and Miss Ann S. Jackson. Bond 5 December 1831. Married
8 December 1831 by George Northam. Sur. and Wit. Franklin Blackburn.
p.106.

BERRY, John D. and Miss Eliza Barrick. Bond 4 December 1834. William
Barrick, father of Eliza. Sur. and Wit. Franklin Blackburn. p. 114.

BERRY, Robert and Lucy Rhodes. Bond 4 November 1773. Sur. and Wit.
Anderson Miller and William Blackburn. p.19.

BERRY, William and Susannah Jackson. Bond 19 December 1788. Married
23 December 1788 by Samuel Klug. Sur. and Wit. William Jackson. p.33.

BERRY, William and Miss Maria Miles. Bond 18 April 1825. William Miles,
deceased, father, and William Harrow, guardian, of Maria. Sur. and Wit.
George Dudley. p.92.

BERRY, William and Miss Martha Ann Deagle. Bond 10 August 1840. William
H. Deagle, Sr., father of Martha. Married 11 August 1840 by Lewis H.
Williams. Sur. and Wit. William H. Deagle. p.120.

BEVEN, Francis and Catherine Carwick. Bond 19 July 1740. Sur. and Wit.
William MacCarty, Richard Corbin, and John Corbin. p.1.

BEVERLEY, Carter and Jane Wormeley. Bond 24 June 1795. Sur. and Wit.
Thomas Churchill and Philip Grymes. p.42.

BIRD, Braxton of King & Queen County and Mary Price, spinster. Bond
18 July 1760. Sur. and Wit. John Price and George Bird. p.12.

BIRD, Major and Miss Lucy Davis, 21 years of age. Bond 21 November 1825.
Alice Davis makes affidavit as to age. Sur. and Wit. James Stamper,
John B. Blake, and Nathaniel W. Bird. p.93.

BIRD, Major and Jane Dudley, over 21 years. Bond 26 May 1847. Married
26 May 1847 by George Northam. Sur. and Wit. Alfred Palmer, Ambrose
R. Bird, and Robert Dudley. p.132.

BIRD, Philemon of Prince Edward County and Mary Lee. Bond 2 November 1762.
Sur. and Wit. James Lee and Benjamin Rhodes. p.14.

BIRD, Richard and [Mary Pamplin.] Bond 9 June 1777. The wife's name not
shown on bond, but written into marriage register. Sur. and Wit.
Robert Pamplin. p.21.

BIRD, Robert and Grace Jefferson (F.N.) Bond 18 March 1840. Married
19 March 1840 by Thomas B. Evans. p.120.

BIRD, William A. and Crissy Cooke. Bond 12 March 1835. Molley Cooke,
mother of Crissy. Sur. and Wit. William Cooke. p.115.

BLACKBURN, Paulin Anderson and Sally Hodges. Bond 10 January 1797.
Married 10 January 1797 by Henry Heffernan. Sur. and Wit. Thomas
Churchill. p.46.

BLACKBURN, P. A. and _____ _____ [wife's name omitted from bond.]
Bond 6 January 1825. Sur. and Wit. Carter Purkins. p.91.

BLACKBURN, Roger and Jane Hackney. Bond 27 December 1779. Elizabeth
Hackney, mother of Jane. Sur. and Wit. Richard Davis and Lusea
Davis. p.23.

BLACKBURN, William S. and Miss Anna H. Miller. Bond 24 February 1845.
Sur. and Wit. William L. Gatewood. p.127.

BLACKLEY, George and Mary Owen. Bond 23 December 1788. Married
25 December 1788 by John Mullins. Sur. and Wit. Thomas Blake. p.33

BLACKLEY, Robert and Frances Batcheldor. Bond 23 November 1761.
Frances is widow of Henry Batcheldor, deceased. Sur. and Wit. Thomas
Whitaker, Ambrose Dudley, John Berry, and Robert Elliot. p.13.

BLACKLEY, Robert C. and Miss Ann C. Thurston. Bond 18 December 1830. Sur.
and Wit. Zedekiah Beddoe. p.105.

BLACKNALL, Charles and Mary Hardin. Bond 3 October 1745. George Hardin,
deceased, father of Mary. Sur. and Wit. Thomas Hardin and Anthony
Smith. p.3.

BLADE, Abraham Currell and Elizabeth Davis. Bond 15 August 1778. Sur.
and Wit. Richard Davis. p.22.

BLADE, Curril and Mary Hanks. Bond 3 July 1792. Sur. and Wit. Isaac
Mercer. p.39.

BLADE, Isaac and Nancy Faulkner. Bond 24 January 1803. Sur. and Wit.
Amos Faulkner and William Wake. p.55.

BLAKE, Augustine and Peggy Marshall. Bond 20 June 1798. Married 23 June
1798 by Henry Heffernan. Sur. and Wit. Robert Long. p.48.

BLAKE, Augustine and Sarah Robinson. Bond 18 December 1799. William
Robinson, father of Sarah. Married 22 December 1799 by Henry
Heffernan. Sur. and Wit. Peter Kemp, Jr. p.50.

BLAKE, Bartlett and Miss Susan Blake. Bond 14 October 1833. Married
17 October 1833 by George Northam. W. C. Blake, guardian of Bartlett.
Sarah Blake, mother of Susan. Sur. and Wit. Robert T. Mountain, Ruben
Blake, and Emerald Walker. p.112.

BLAKE, Benjamin of Gloucester County and Mrs. Betty Stiff, widow. Bond
1 January 1805. Married 2 January 1805 by Argyle W. White. Sur. and
Wit. Vincent Yarrington and Elizabeth B. Yarrington. p.59.

BLAKE, Berkeley Saunders and Elizabeth Robinson Blake. Bond 11 September
1807. Married 17 September 1807 by David Corey. Sur. and Wit. Warner
Blake. p.64.

BLAKE, Beverley A. and Miss Nancy Read. Bond __ July 1807. Married
15 July 1807 by Henry Heffernan. Sur. and Wit. Edmund Read. p.64.

BLAKE, George and Chrisse Saunders. Bond 20 March 1781. Thomas Saunders,
father of Chrisse. Sur. and Wit. Jacob Stiff Saunders. p.24.

BLAKE, George and Betty Saunders. Bond 12 July 1785. Married 14 July
1785 by Samuel Klug. Sur. and Wit. Thomas Saunders, Jr. p.28.

BLAKE, George and Mary Brummell. Bond 4 February 1786. Elizabeth Brummell
gives consent for her daughter. Sur. and Wit. John Blake and George
West. p.29.

BLAKE, George and Mrs. Caroline Newcomb. Bond 24 December 1845. Married
25 December 1845 by R. A. Christian. Sur. and Wit. Norborne C. Sibley
and B. B. Sibley. p.129.

BLAKE, Jacob S. and Julian D. Sibley. Bond 13 May 1817. Daniel B. Sibley,
father of Julian. Sur. and Wit. Daniel B. Sibley. p.83.

BLAKE, Jacob S. and Lucy Blake. Bond 27 January 1845. Married 4 February
1845 by George Northam. George Blake, father of Lucy. Sur. and Wit.
Benjamin B. Sibley and J. W. Daniel. p.127.

BLAKE, James and Kesiah A. Duncan. Married 3 December 1835 by George
Northam. [Minister's return only.] p.160.

BLAKE, John and Elizabeth Baker. Bond 24 April 1753. Sur. and Wit.
William Healy and Leonard Hill. p.7.

BLAKE, John and Lucy Blake. Bond 5 December 1759. John Blake, father
of Lucy. Sur. and Wit. James Gibson. p.11.

BLAKE, John and Alice Hackney. Bond 17 November 1773. William Hackney,
father of Alice. Sur. and Wit. Jonathan McNikal. p.19.

BLAKE, John and Joanna Long. Bond 3 June 1824. Robert Long, father of
Joanna. Sur. and Wit. George Walker. p.89.

BLAKE, John B. and Nancy G. Miller. Bond 22 January 1827. Sur. and Wit.
Robert N. Blake. p.96.

BLAKE, Robert and Miss Ann Elizabeth Miller. Bond 13 October 1832.
Isham Miller, deceased, and Nancy Miller, parents of Ann. Sur. and
Wit. John B. Blake and Rebecca Dunlevy. p.109.

BLAKE, Robert Miller, age 26 years, single, born in Middlesex, son of
John B. and Nancy G. Blake, and Sarah E. Neal, single, daughter of
James and Susan Neal. Married 22 December 1854 by Holland Walker at
John B. Blake's. p.170.

BLAKE, Robert N. and Letitia Boldry. Bond 19 November 1798. Married
20 November 1798 by Henry Heffernan. Sur. and Wit. Benjamin Hackney
and Christopher Blackburn. p.48.

BLAKE, Robert N. and Emerald Walker. Married 30 March 1841 by George
Northam. [Minister's return only.] p.162.

BLAKE, Samuel and Sarah Wood. Bond 17 September 1798. Married 20 September 1798 by Henry Heffernan. Sur. and Wit. William Wood. p.48.

BLAKE, Thomas and Crissy Miller. Bond 1 April 1790. Married 10 April
1790 by John Mullins. Sur. and Wit. George Dillard. p.35.

BLAKE, Thomas and Miss Elizabeth Stamper. Bond 29 January 1816. John
Stamper, deceased, father of Elizabeth. Sur. and Wit. Mathew Major.
p.80.

BLAKE, Thomas D. and Miss Ann H. Sibley. Bond 3 January 1825. Sur. and
Wit. William S. Robinson and Hierom Walker. p.91.

BLAKE, Warner C. and Miss Sarah Blake, 21 years of age. Bond 10 December
1810. Sur. and Wit. James Stiff. p.71.

BLAKE, William and Rachel Williams. Bond 1 November 1773. Benjamin
Williams, father of Rachel. Sur. and Wit. John Morgan, Benjamin
Churchhill, and William Pace. p.19.

BLAKE, William S. and Miss Cordelia Blake. Bond 20 December 1831. Married
29 December 1831 by George Northam. Sur. and Wit. Samuel Blake. p.107.

BLAKE, Zachariah J. and Mary L. Blake. Married 24 December 1841 by George
Northam. [Minister's return only.] p.162.

BLAKEY, Churchhill and Ann Chowning. Bond 15 October 1772. Sur. and Wit.
William Taylor. p.17.

BLAKEY, George and Catherine Shelton. Bond 31 December 1743. Sur. and
Wit. Robert Daniel and Thomas Price. p.2.

BLAKEY, George of Spotsylvania County and Clara Daniel, widow. Bond
28 April 1746. Sur. and Wit. Robert George of Caroline County. p.3.

BLAKEY, Henry and Frances O. George. Bond 28 August 1802. John George,Jr.
father of Frances. Married 29 August 1802 by Henry Heffernan. Sur.
and Wit. Thomas Kidd, James Owen, and Elizabeth Meacham. p.54.

BLAKEY, John C. and Adeline Evans. Bond 4 October 1847. Married in
October 1847 by Thomas B. Evans. Sur. and Wit. Richard A. Davis,
Thomas B. Evans, and Lafayette Evans. p.132.

BLAKEY, Robert and Miss Frances Daniel Roane. Bond 12 October 1808.
John Quarles, guardian of Frances. Sur. and Wit. Thomas Muse, Jr.,
James Baytop, Catharine Baytop, and Neilson Muse. p.67.

BLAKEY, William C. and Jane Healy. Bond 27 January 1802. Married
28 January 1802 by Henry Heffernan. Thomas Healy, father of Jane.
Sur. and Wit. James Healy. p.54.

BOHANNON, Joseph and Elizabeth Hunley. Bond 29 November 1797. Sur. and
Wit. William Hudgin. p.47.

BOSS, Albert A. and Maria Adeline Daniels. Bond 23 June 1851. Married
25 June 1851 by Zach Street. M. Daniel, parent of Maria. Sur. and
Wit. John A. Jesse and W. H. Groom. p.140.

BOSS, James and Susan Powell. Bond 3 September 1788. Married 1 September 1788 by Samuel Klug. Sur. and Wit. David Powell. p.33.

BOSS, John and Judith Faulkner. Bond 12 December 1774. Sur. and Wit.
Will Churchhill. p.20.

BOSS, John and Ann Jackson. Bond 3 May 1796. Married 4 May 1796 by
Henry Heffernan. John Jackson, father of Ann. Sur. and Wit. William
Jackson. p.45.

BOSS, John and Miss Mahala Kellum. Bond 17 May 1819. Thomas Healy,
guardian of John, and Abel Kellum, father of Mahala. Sur. and Wit.
Thomas Edwards. p.84.

BOSS, John and _____ _____ [name omitted]. Bond 27 December 1824.
Sur. and Wit. Nat. Healy. p.91.

BOSS, John B. and Miss Sarah Lewis. Bond 29 December 1832. Sur. and
Wit. James S. Bristow. p.110.

BOSS, John B. and Miss Mary Honsday. Bond 21 December 1843. Married
21 December 1843 by Richard A. Christian. Sur. and Wit. Larkin S.
Bristow and Sarah E. R. Owen. p.124.

BOSS, John J. and [Ann Berry.] Bond 27 December 1824. Married 29 December 1824 by Richard Claybrook. The wife's name was not shown on
bond, but was given in the Minister's return. Sur. and Wit. John D.
Berry. p.90.

BOSS, John, Jr. and Sally Scott. Bond 28 May 1792. Married 28 May
1792 by John Mullins. Sur. and Wit. William Hill. p.38.

BOSS, Joseph and Elizabeth Barrick. Bond 21 December 1792. Sur. and
Wit. George West. p.39.

BOSS, Lewis and Mary Atkinson. Bond 26 October 1792. Married 28 October 1792 by John Mullins. Sur. and Wit. Leonard Atkinson and Christopher Robinson. p.39.

BOSS, Lewis and Sally Parker. Bond 18 November 1795. Married 13 December 1795 by John Healy. Sur. and Wit. James Hopkins. p.44.

BOSS, Meacham C. and Susanna Sibley. Bond 17 April 1817. Thomas Sibley, deceased, father of Susanna. Sur. and Wit. James W. Dunlevy. p.82.

BOSS, William and Sarah Bayton. Bond 19 June 1790. Married 26 June 1790 by John Mullins. Sur. and Wit. Lewis Boss. p.36.

BROOKS, Broughton and Ann B. Seward. Bond 15 December 1827. Married 15 December 1827 by Richard Claybrook. Lewis Seward, father of Ann. Sur. and Wit. Lewis Seward. p.98.

BOULWARE, Muscoe and Martha G. Healy. Married 23 December 1841 by Richard A. Christian. [Minister's return only.] p.164.

BOWDEN, William and Sarah Owen. Bond 8 December 1779. Sur. and Wit. William Owen. p.23.

BOWDEN, William and Jane Dudley. Bond 26 April 1794. Married 27 April 1794 by Richard Bassett. Sur. and Wit. William Layton. p.41.

BRAME, Josiah and Sarah Richardson. Bond 7 December 1762. Sarah is widow of James Richardson. Sur. and Wit. James Daniel and William Moulson. p.14.

BRAME, Leonard and Ruth Kidd. Married 10 May 1794 by John Healy. [Minister's return only.] p.150

BRAXTON, Carter and Miss Judith Robinson, spinster. Bond 16 July 1755. Humphrey Hill and John Robinson, guardians of Carter. Sur. and Wit. Christopher Robinson, Esq., Walker Taliaferro, George Braxton, and John Symmer. p.9.

BRAXTON, Carter and Miss Mary Grymes Sayre. Bond 21 May 1823. Married 21 May 1823 by Jonathan Silliman, New Kent County. Samuel Will Sayre, father of Mary. Sur. and Wit. Samuel Wil. Sayre. p.87.

BRAXTON, Thomas C. and Miss Maria G. Davis. Bond 14 December 1814. C. H. Braxton, guardian of Thomas. Staige Davis, deceased, father of Maria. Sur. and Wit. Henry M. Didlake and Peyton Grymes. p.78.

BRAY, Elliott and Sarah E. Bristow. Bond 30 May 1839. Married 30 May 1839 by George Northam. Sur. and Wit. Thomas R. Sutton. p.118.

BRAY, James and Frances Thacker. Bond 23 July 1740. Sur. and Wit. John Walker and Christopher Curtis. p.1.

BRAY, John and Miss Elizabeth Bristow. Bond 25 December 1815. Sur and Wit. Leonard Bristow. p.80.

BRAY, Robert and Mary E. Healy. Bond 24 August 1835. Elizabeth O. Healy, mother of Mary. Sur. and Wit. George W. Major and John P. Bristow. p.116.

BRAY, Thomas and Polly Bristow. Bond 16 February 1789. Married 21 February 1789 by Samuel Klug. Sur. and Wit. Josiah Bristow. p.34.

BRAY, Thomas M. and Ophelia Maderis. Bond 6 February 1852. Married 7 February 1852 by Zach Street. Sur. and Wit. Thomas F. Taff. p.141.

BRIANT, Robert and Miss Elizabeth French. Bond 18 January 1826. Sur. and Wit. Thomas J. Palmer and William Barick. p.94.

BRIANT, Robert and Miss Susannah Boss. Bond 20 January 1835. Married 22 January 1835 by George Northam. Sur. and Wit. James Barrick and John C. New. p.115.

BRIM, Leonard and Miss Nancy Jacobs. Bond 5 June 1825. Sur. and Wit. H. Thruston. p.92.

BRIMM, John and Miss Eliza Kidd. Bond 18 December 1833. Sur. and Wit. Curtis Wood. p.113.

BRISTOW, Alexander and Frances Guthrie. Bond 28 May 1781. Sur. and Wit. Griffin Tuggle. p.25.

BRISTOW, Alexander and Elizabeth Knowles. Bond 23 April 1794. Sur. and Wit. George Atkins. p.41.

BRISTOW, Alexander and Nancy Brown, single and above 21 years. Bond 9 August 1806. Married 9 August 1806 by Henry Heffernan. Sur. and Wit. James Kidd, John Chew, and Mary Watson. p.62.

BRISTOW, Bartholomew and Ann Saunders. Bond 28 March 1786. Sur. and Wit. George Saunders. p.30.

BRISTOW, Bartholomew and Elizabeth Bristow. Bond 20 May 1791. Married 22 May 1791 by John Mullins. Sur. and Wit. James Healy. p.37.

BRISTOW, Benjamin and Sarah Lister. Bond 19 November 1773. Sur. and Wit. William Jones and William Dawson. p.19.

BRISTOW, Benjamin and Ann Saunders. Bond 5 January 1795. Married 6 January 1795 by Armistead Smith, who shows the wife's name as Nancy Saunders. Sur. and Wit. Benjamin Hackney. p.42.

BRISTOW, Henry and Elizabeth Frances Beddoo. Bond 4 October 1848. Married in October 1848 by Thomas B. Evans. Lucy Fowler gives consent for Elizabeth. Sur. and Wit. Thomas M. Bray and Virginia J. Walden. p.135.

BRISTOW, James B. and Rebecca Seward. Bond 6 November 1805. Henry Mickelburrough, guardian of Rebecca. Sur. and Wit. Henry Mickelburrough. p.60.

BRISTOW, James S. and Leonora Seward. Bond 24 December 1832. Ann Bristow consents for her son. Sur. and Wit. Lewis S. Bristow and George W. Major. p.110.

BRISTOW, John and Frances Brooks. Bond 30 January 1779. Sur. and Wit. Benjamin Bristow. p.22.

BRISTOW, John and Nancy Walden. Bond 24 January 1812. Lewis Walden, father of Nancy. Sur. and Wit. Taliaferro Hunter. p.73.

BRISTOW, John and Mary Watson. Bond 27 January 1808. Married 31 January 1808 by Henry Heffernan. Mary is widow of Robert Watson. Sur. and Wit. Beverly Daniel. p.66.

BRISTOW, John, widower and Mrs. Polley Sears. Bond 14 November 1813. Polley is widow of John Sears. Sur. and Wit. George Healy and James Kidd. p.76.

BRISTOW, John P., over 21, and Mary Ann St. John. Bond 15 December 1823. William St. John, deceased, father of Mary Ann. Nancy St. John, guardian of her daughter. Sur. and Wit. Edmond Healy. p.86.

BRISTOW, Josiah and Elizabeth Wilkins. Bond 24 January 1781. Sur. and Wit. William Churchhill. p.24.

BRISTOW, Josiah and Fanny Bristow. Bond 22 December 1786. Married 24 December 1786 by Samuel Klug. Sur. and Wit. Benjamin Bristow. p.30.

BRISTOW, Leonard and Lucy Seward. Bond 12 December 1797. Sur. and Wit. Thomas Bray and Churchill Blackburn. p.47.

BRISTOW, Lewis S. and Miss Frances St. John. Bond 7 November 1825. William St. John, deceased, father of Frances. Nancy St. John, guardian of her daughter. p.93.

BRISTOW, Richard H. and Lucy Ann Bray. Married 15 April 1841 by Richard A. Christian. [Minister's return only.] p.164.

BRISTOW, Richard H. and Frances A. South. Bond 1 June 1850. Sur. and Wit. John L. Johnson. p.138.

BRISTOW, Samuel, of Surry County, and Anne Guthery. Bond 1 January 1765. Sur. and Wit. James Berry and Christopher Robinson. p.15.

BRISTOW, Sanders and Sarah Smith. Bond 26 March 1781. Sur. and Wit. Benjamin Kidd. p.24.

BRISTOW, Saunders and Nancy Crossfield. Bond 12 August 1788. Married 17 August 1788 by Samuel Klug. Sur. and Wit. Thomas Blake and William Churchill. p.33.

BRISTOW, Saunders and Jane Lee. Bond 13 November 1799. Sur. and Wit. Griffin Tuggle and Peter Kemp, Jr. p.50.

BRISTOW, Thomas S. and Miss Fanny Moore. Bond 7 May 1829. Married between 2 July 1828 and 2 July 1829 by Nathan Healy. Sur. and Wit. George L. Moore. p.101.

BRISTOW, Thomas S. and Mary Garrett. Bond 27 January 1840. Married 31 January 1840 by Thomas B. Evans. Sur. and Wit. Richard Garrett. p.119.

BRISTOW, Thomas S. and Miss Eudora Bristow, 21 years of age. Bond 10 May 1848. Married on __ May 1848 by Thomas B. Evans. Sur. and Wit. Richard H. Bristow and William R. Pike. p.134.

BRISTOW, Walter and Agnes Garrett. Bond 28 December 1847. Married 28 December 1847 by R. A. Christian. Richard Garrett gives affidavit that Agnes is of age. Sur. and Wit. Thomas A. Dix and Richard Garrett. p.133.

BRISTOW, William and Jane Ware. Bond 23 May 1796. Sur. and Wit. Bartholomew Bristow. p. 45.

BRISTOW, William and Miss Agnes Garrett. Bond 8 April 1814. Sur. and Wit. Bartholomew Bristow. p.76.

BRISTOW, Zachariah W. and _____ _____. Bond 27 December 1824. [wife's name omitted from bond.] Sur. and Wit. Henry Thruston. p.91.

BRIZENDINE, Wiley and Miss Sarah Owen. Bond 19 December 1843. Polly Owen, mother of Sarah. Sur. and Wit. Joseph Owen, Henry Johnson, and Isaac N. Mercer. p.124.

BROADWATER, James and Eliza Ann Boss. Bond 24 April 1848. Married 24 April 1848 by R. A. Christian. Sur. and Wit. Robert Healy. p.134.

BROOCKE, Benjamin and Elizabeth Seward. Bond 22 December 1834. Lewis Seward, father of Elizabeth. Sur. and Wit. Lewis Seward. p.115.

BROOK or BROOCKE, Lewis and Miss Elizabeth Blake. Bond 27 December 1809. William Broocke, father of Lewis. Thomas Blake, father of Elizabeth. Sur. and Wit. Thomas Blake. p.69.

BROOKE, Christopher, of King & Queen County, and Elizabeth Saunders. Bond 23 December 1782. Sur. and Wit. Isaac Digges, George Saunders, and Frances Digges. p.26.

BROOKING, William and Betty L. Daniel. Bond 28 August 1792. Charles Lee, guardian of Betty. Sur. and Wit. Thomas Robinson and James Webb. p.39.

BROOKS, James and Miss Frances Wood. Bond 23 November 1812. William Wood, deceased, father of Frances. Sur. and Wit. Robert Barrick. p.75.

BROOKS, John and Ann Mickelburrough. Bond 22 April 1779. Sur. and Wit. George Dillard. p.22.

BROOKS, Samuel and Priscilla Piper. Bond 26 October 1778. Sur. and Wit. Benjamin Williams. p.22.

BROOKS, Samuel, Jr. and Sarah Williamson. Bond 2 January 1816. Sarah is widow of Benjamin Williamson, deceased. Sur. and Wit. Thomas Groom. p. 80.

BROOKS, Thomas, whose parents live in Essex County, and Ann Johnson, orphan. Bond 13 May 1785. Elliott Sturman, with whom Ann lives, gives consent. Sur. and Wit. John Richards. p.28.

BROWN, Charles and Catharine Hackney, of age. Bond 7 July 1797. Married 8 July 1797 by Henry Heffernan. William and Sarah Hackney, parents of Catharine. Sur. and Wit. Isaac Jones, Churchill Blackburn, Gabriel Jones, and Benjamin Hackney. p.46.

BROWN, James and Judith Yarrington. Bond 30 September 1752. Judith was born 6 August 1728, from Register of S. Farnham by Alexander Cruden, and daughter of Massey and Ann Yarrington. Sur. and Wit. William Cardwell, John Walton, and John Griggs. p.6.

BROWN, James, of James City County, and Catherine Cheney. Bond 25 April 1764. Sur. and Wit. Joseph Tuggle, Elizabeth Elliot, and John Elliot. p.15.

BROWN, John and Mary Bennett, of age. Bond 22 October 1805. James Owen, stepfather of Mary. Winney Owen gives affidavit as to Mary's age. Sur. and Wit. James Owen and Bartholomew Bristow. P.60.

BROWN, John B. and Miss Mildred Reveer, 21 years of age. Bond 25 August 1845. Married 25 August 1845 by Richard A. Christian. Sur. and Wit. R. A. Davis and Adline Reveer. p.129.

BROWN, Smith and Susan Garrett. Married 7 October 1841 by Richard A. Christian. [Minister's return only.] p.164.

BROWN, Thomas S. and Miss Mary Burns. Bond 15 January 1834. Sur. and Wit. George Moore. p.113.

BROWN, Thomas and Miss Judith E. Daniel. Bond 10 July 1843. Sur. and Wit. George B. Daniel. p.123.

BUCKNER, John and Dorothy Scrosby. Bond 23 November 1785. Married 24 November 1785 by Samuel Klug. Sur. and Wit. William Churchhill. p.28.

BULL, Thomas R. and Miss Mary Anna Miles. Bond 12 December 1843. Married 27 December 1843 by George Northam. Robert Healy, guardian of Mary. Sur. and Wit. John J. Burke. p.124.

BUNDICK, John and Sarah Ann Mears. Bond 2 January 1843. Married 4 January 1843 by George Northam. William Mears, deceased, father of Sarah; Charles Berry, her guardian. Sur. and Wit. Edward Topping, James H. White, Henry B. White, and Warren W. C. Pool. p.122.

BUNDICK, John and Miss Alcie Watts. Bond 1 January 1844. James Watts, father of Alcie. Sur. and Wit. James B. Barrick and Thomas Wyatt. p.124.

BURCH, James and Elizabeth McKan. Bond 28 January 1793. Married 28 January 1793 by John Mullins. Sur. and Wit. John McKan. p.40.

BURK, Thomas and Susanna Blake. Bond 10 February 1783. Sur. and Wit. Jacob Blake, Elizabeth Miller, and Jacob Blake. p.26.

BURK, Thomas and Elizabeth Sutton. Bond 5 March 1787. Married 8 March 1787 by Samuel Klug. Sur. and Wit. Charles Dudley. p.31.

BURKE, William and Mrs. Sarah R. Grymes. Bond 3 January 1827. Married 3 January 1827 by Richard Claybrook. Sarah is widow of Philip Grymes, deceased. Sur. and Wit. George Healy. p.96.

BURKE, William M. and Miss Polly H. Berry. Bond 22 March 1813. William Berry, deceased, father of Polly. Sur. and Wit. H. Hudgin. p.76.

BURNS, George and Ann Callehan. Bond 2 January 1805. Married 3 January 1805 by Argyle W. White. Sur. and Wit. John B. Garland and Benjamin Blake. p.59.

BURNS, Josiah and Mary Garland. Bond 26 November 1800. Married 29 November 1800 by Henry Heffernan. David Garland, father of Mary. Sur. and Wit. David Garland. p.51.

BURTON, John and Mary Blade. Bond 8 February 1797. Married 19 March 1797 by Henry Heffernan. Sur. and Wit. Dudley Vaughan. p.46.

BURTON, Simon and Nancy Robinson. Bond 28 December 1790. William Robinson gives consent. Sur. and Wit. William Robinson. p.36.

BURWELL, Lewis, Esq. of James City County, and Mrs. Frances Bray, widow. Bond 21 January 1745. Sur. and Wit. Henry Thacker. p.3.

BURWELL, Nathaniel, of James City County, and Susanna Grymes. Bond 28 November 1772. Sur. and Wit. Philip Grymes and Will Churchhill. p.17.

BUSH, John and Jane Good. Bond 13 October 1788. Married 6 November 1788 by Samuel Klug. Sur. and Wit. William Goode and Peter Kemp. p.33.

BUTLER, Thomas and Elizabeth Bowcock. Bond 25 November 1793. Married 18 December 1793 by John Mullins. Sur. and Wit. Samuel Ware and John Clarke. p.41.

CADE, Nelson P. and Miss Catharine Trice. Bond 18 October 1844. Sur. and Wit. James W. Games. p.126.

CALLIS, John W., of Mathews County, and Miss Virginia Ann Gibson. Married 24 October 1837 by L. W. Allen. [Minister's return only.] p.164.

CAMPBELL, Alexander and Elizabeth M. Healy. Bond 18 December 1848. Married 21 December 1848 by R. A. Christian. A.G.D.Roy, guardian of Alexander. W. Healy, father of Elizabeth. Sur. and Wit. Andrew C. Browne. p.135.

CARDWELL, John and Elizabeth Stamper. Bond 25 February 1783. Sur. and Wit. Richard Cardwell. p.27.

CARLTON, Benjamin F. and Ann Maderis. Bond 10 June 1846. Sur. and Wit. John P. Dunn, John A. Carlton, and Henry Dickerson. p.130.

CARLTON, John R. and Miss Sarah McKan. This is consent only, which was incomplete and signed by John Street. p.143.

CARLTON, Will E. and Miss Martha Owen, of age. Bond 4 June 1832. Mrs. Polly Owen, mother of Martha. Sur. and Wit. John Owen and Alfred Healy. p.108.

CARNEY, George M. and Jane Humphries. Bond 12 June 1824. Nelson Humphries, deceased, father of Jane. Sur. and Wit. Moses Walker, Jr. p.89.

CARTER, George and Catharine Brown, widow. Bond 28 November 1803. Married 28 November 1803 by William Fritchett of Mathews County. Sur. and Wit. David Corey and William Tomanson. p.57.

CARTER, George A. and Sarah F. Palmer. Bond 8 December 1848. Married 14 December 1848 by Holland Walker. Thomas J. Palmer, father of Sarah. Sur. and Wit. George F. Blackburn. p.135.

CARTER, Dr. Robert O. and Edmonia Fauntleroy Corbin. Bond 30 September 1845. Married 30 September 1845 by Richard A. Christian. Richard R. Corbin, father of Edmonia. Sur. and Wit. Thomas W. Fauntleroy. p.129.

CARTER, Thomas and Elizabeth Meaderis. Bond 9 October 1787. Sur. and Wit. Thomas Farguson. p.31.

CASSITY, James, free mulatto, and Lucy Martin, free mulatto. Bond 11 December 1810. Nancy Martin, mother of Lucy. Sur. and Wit. Joseph Boss and James Parker. p.71.

CAUTHORN, Pearson and Mrs. Maria E. Segar. Bond 22 November 1843. Sur. and Wit. John J. Muse and William L. Gatewood. p.124.

CHAPMAN, Henry and Miss Sarah C. Bristow. Bond 2 February 1826. Sur. and Wit. Nathan Healy. p.94.

CAUTHORN, Leroy and Ann Y. Montague, above 21 years. Bond 16 February 1807. Catherine Cauthorn gives consent. Sur. and Wit. William Parson, James Dunn, and Amos Cauthorn. p.63.

CHARLES, Lewis and Miss Jane Brim. Bond 27 April 1829. Sur. and Wit. Leonard Brim. p. 101.

CHARLES, Travis and Lucy Sears. Bond 26 October 1795. Sur. and Wit. John Daniel and William Jones. p.43.

CHINN, John and Sarah Yates, spinster. Bond 20 February 1765. Sur. and Wit. Overton Cosby and Ja. Gregorie. p.16.

CHOWNING, Henry and Margaret Allen. Bond 7 September 1785. Married 11 September 1785 by Samuel Klug. Sur. and Wit. Tobias Allen. p.28.

CHOWNING, James and Miss Maria Sutton. Bond 2 June 1810. John Sutton, deceased, father of Maria; Staige Davis, guardian. Sur. and Wit. Staige Davis. p.70.

CHOWNING, James and Miss Elizabeth H. Whiting. Bond 19 October 1825. Married 14 October 1825 by Richard Claybrook. Sur. and Wit. William Jesse, Susan S. Whiting, and Ann A. Foster. p.93.

CHOWNING, James and Ann C. D. Games. Married 29 December 1835 by Joseph Goodman. William Games, deceased, father of Ann; Colonel William Shepherd, guardian. [Minister's return only.] p.160.

CHOWNING, John and Catharine Chowning. Bond 15 July 1774. Sur. and Wit. William Chowning. p.20.

CHOWNING, John and Catharine Blakey. Married 4 December 1804 by Henry Heffernan. [Minister's return only.] p.155.

CHOWNING, John, Jr. and Mrs. Elizabeth Robinson. Bond 16 May 1812. Sur. and Wit. William Jesse, Margaret Harper, Ann C. Street, Deborah E. C. Robinson, and Christopher Owen. p.74

CHOWNING, Robert and Fanny Abbott. Bond 27 December 1788. Married 1 January 1789 by Samuel Klug. Sur. and Wit. William Kidd and Thomas Iverson. p.33.

CHOWNING, Robert and Catharine Groom. Bond 26 January 1795. Married on 7 February 1795 by Robert Ware. Sur. and Wit. Thomas Saunders. p.42.

CHOWNING, Thomas and Elizabeth George. Bond 24 May 1784. Sur. and Wit. Leonard George. p.27.

CHRISTIAN, Joseph and Maria A. Healy (M. Augusta Healy). Bond 25 June 1850. Married in June 1850 by Thomas B. Evans. Sur. and Wit. Robert N. Trice and J. H. Muse. p.139.

CHRISTIAN, Patrick A. and Tabitha Christian, of lawful age. Bond 17 December 1825. Sur. and Wit. Richard A. Christian. p.93.

CHRISTOPHER, James and Miss Nancy Hart. Bond 13 March 1824. Richard Hart, father of Nancy. Sur. and Wit. Thomas Fitzgerald. p.89.

CHRISTOPHER, John and Elizabeth Anderton, 21 years of age. Bond 7 February 1825. William Anderton, deceased, father of Elizabeth. Sur. and Wit. John G. Anderton and George Northam. p.91.

CHRISTOPHER, Nathan H. and Mary J. Peade. Bond 24 March 1852. Sur. and Wit. Thomas S. Hall. p.141.

CHRISTOPHER, Riley and Fama Ann Stant. Bond 26 September 1846. Married __ September 1846 by John J. Boss. Susan Christopher, mother of Riley. Sur. and Wit. George W. Revel, John R. Creighton, and R. H. Crittenden. p.131.

CHRISTOPHER, Thomas and Miss Susannah Hart. Bond 28 March 1825. Richard Hart, father of Susannah. Sur. and Wit. William Ailworth and Ransom Greenwood. p.92.

CHRISTOPHER, William and Frances Norton. Bond 23 October 1833. Frances is widow of Thomas Norton, deceased. Sur. and Wit. William R. Pace. p.112.

CHURCHILL, Thomas and Elizabeth B. Berkeley. Bond 26 May 1801. Married 28 May 1801 by Henry Heffernan. Edmund Berkeley, Esq., father of Elizabeth. Sur. and Wit. John Chew, Jr. p. 53.

CHURCHILL, Thomas and Lucy B. Lilly, over 21 years. Bond 13 July 1803. Sur. and Wit. Samuel Harris. p.56.

CLARE, John and Miss Lucy Dudley. Bond 1 July 1760. Sur. and Wit. John Berry. p.12.

CLARE, John and Rosetta Jones. Bond 6 January 1830. Married 7 January 1830 by George Northam. Robert Barrick, guardian of Rosetta. Sur. and Wit. Robert Barrick. p.102.

CLARE, Robert and Miss Elizabeth M. Humphries. Bond 17 March 1829. Married 18 March 1829 by George Northam. Sur. and Wit. Edmund Stiff and Polly D. Stiff. p.101.

CLARE, Thomas and Martha Barnrick. Bond 28 January 1786. Sur. and Wit. Thomas Barnrick. p.29.

CLARE (CLAIR), Thomas and Miss Eliza Atkinson. Bond 23 February 1813. James Healy, Jr., guardian of Eliza. Sur. and Wit. George W. Layton and John H. Saunders. p.76.

CLARE, Thomas H. and Miss Elizabeth Goode. Bond 10 July 1843. Sur. and Wit. William N. Walker and William L. Gatewood. p.123.

CLARE (CLEAR), William and Mrs. Frances Brooke. Bond 21 April 1830. Married 28 April 1830 by George Northam. Sur. and Wit. John Clare. p.103.

CLARK, George A. and Mary Ann Cundieff. Married 29 December 1842 by George Northam. [Minister's return only.] p.162.

CLARK, John and Mary Yarrington. Bond 29 September 1782. John Yarrington, father of Mary. Sur. and Wit. William Jeffries, John Clark, Sr., and Henry Brooks. p.26.

CLARK, Spencer and Nancy Claudas. Bond 23 April 1787. Married 26 May 1787 by Samuel Klug. Sur. and Wit. Richard Montague and J. Shackelford. p.31.

CLARKE, Braxton and Mrs. Mary M. Wood. Bond 26 March 1834. Mary is widow of James W. Wood, deceased. Sur. and Wit. Robert T. Mountain. p.114.

CLARKE, Lewis and Miss Maria Jane Crosswell. Bond 1 January 1845. Married 9 January 1845 by George Northam. Sur. and Wit. Robert C. Garland. p.127.

CLARKE, Lewis and Elizabeth S. Smith. Bond 9 February 1846. Married 10 February 1846 by George Northam. Sur. and Wit. William D. Turner and John L. Mercer. p.130.

CLARKE, Spencer and Mrs. Elizabeth Mercer. Bond 2 November 1807. Married 2 November 1807 by David Corey. [Another return by Mr. Corey states they were married on the 19 November 1807.] Sur. and Wit. Christopher Owen, George Blake, and John Daniel. p.65.

CLARKE, Theoderick and Miss Frances Daniel. Bond 17 November 1807. Sur. and Wit. Christopher Owen. p.65.

CLARKE, Thomas, Jr. and Mrs. Molly McKan, widow of Philip McKan. Bond 26 August 1811. Sur. and Wit. William Clarke and Richard Jones. p.72.

CLARKE, William and Mrs. Lucy McKan. Bond 10 February 1812. Sur. and Wit. Richard Jones and Peter Taff. p.74.

CLAYBROOKE Richard and Miss Julia D. Shepherd. Bond 1 October 1811. Married 5 October 1811 by Philip Montague. Henry D. Shepherd, deceased, father of Julia; Joseph Godwin, her guardian. Sur. and Wit. Joseph Godwin. p. 72.

CLAYTON, Jasper S. and Mary Berkeley. Bond 29 January 1806. Sur. and Wit. James Spark. p.61.

CLOUDAS, Abner and Sarah Daniel. Bond 27 March 1782. Sur. and Wit. John Daniel. p.25.

CLOUDAS, Absolam and Miss Frances Trice, 21 years of age. Bond 17 July 1810. Ned Trice, father of Frances. Sur. and Wit. Thomas Trice. p.70.

CLOUDAS, Beverley and Frances Montague. Bond 23 May 1791. Married 25 May 1791 by John Mullins. Sur. and Wit. John Beaman and Thomas Iverson. p.37.

CLOUDAS, Elliott and Anne C. Daniel. Bond 28 May 1823. Robert Daniel, Sr., father of Anne. Sur. and Wit. Robert Daniel, Sr. p.87.

COATES, Robert and Miss Mary Rilee, of age. Bond 25 February 1834. Sur. and Wit. John Lewis. p.113.

COLE, Samuel and Maria Berry. Married 18 October 1837 by George Northam. [Minister's return only.] p.161.

COLLINS, Robert and Martha Jane Gibson. Bond 23 May 1836. John Gibson, father of Martha. Sur. and Wit. John Gibson. p.116.

COLLINS, William and Caroline Sears. Bond 7 April 1849. Married in April 1849 by Thomas B. Evans, who has (F.N.) on his return. The father of Caroline gives consent, but his name not mentioned. p. 136.

COLLINS, Zachariah and Ann Burton. Bond 20 December 1797. Married 21 December 1797 by Henry Heffernan. Sur. and Wit. Dudley Vaughan. p.47.

COLMARY, Abraham, over 21 years, and Jane Elizabeth Cundiff. Bond 22 October 1839. Ann S. Cundiff, mother of Jane. Sur. and Wit. Esra R. H. Bennett. p.119.

CONGROWS, Moses and Susanna Boughton, spinster. Bond 12 April 1799. Mary Boughton, mother of Susanna. Sur. and Wit. Bivvin Abbott, John Baytop, Richard Boughton, J. H. T. Lorimer, and W. Boughton. p.49.

COOK, Thomas, of Gloucester, and Rachel Murray Beverley Yates. Bond 11 January 1798. Married 15 January 1799 by Henry Heffernan. [The consent was dated 10 January 1799.] Thomas Roane, guardian of Rachel. Sur. and Wit. George Murray. p. 47.

COOKE, James and Mary Goalman, free people of color. Bond 13 June 1832. George Goalman, father of Mary. Sur. and Wit. George W. Palmer. p.108.

COOKE, Mordecia and Elizabeth Scrosby. Bond 17 December 1781. Robert Matthews, guardian of Elizabeth. Sur. and Wit. Simon Laughlin. p.25.

COOKE, Richard and Elizabeth Blueford. Bond 5 September 1795. Married 6 September 1795 by Henry Heffernan. Sur. and Wit. Thomas Churchill and Christopher Robinson. p.43.

COOKE, Thomas and Catharine B. Didlake. Bond 16 January 1806. Married 16 January 1806 by Henry Heffernan. James Didlake, deceased, father of Catharine. Sur. and Wit. Staige Davis. p.61.

COOKE, William and Polly Maggs. Bond 27 December 1805. Mordecai Cooke of Gloucester County gives affidavit that William Cooke is a free man. Sur. and Wit. James Maggs. p.60.

COOPER, William and Miss Anna Farrow. Bond 16 February 1829. Sur. and Wit. James Dunn, Henry Mederias, and George T. R. Healy. p.101

COPPER, Richard and Lucy E. Brooks, both 21 years. Bond 19 September 1840. Sur. and Wit. Elliott Gardner, Thomas Trice and Jane W. Trice. p.121

CORBIN, John Tayloe and Juliet Muse. Bond 26 January 1799. Married 31 January 1799 by Henry Heffernan. Hudson Muse, father of Juliet, gives consent. Sur. and Wit. Thomas Muse, Jr. p.49.

CORBIN, Richard Henry and Betty Tayloe. Married 10 February 1797 by
Henry Heffernan, out of the county. [Minister's return only.] p.152.

CORBIN, Richard Randolph, Esq. and Miss Catherine Fauntleroy. Bond
28 May 1821. Thomas Fauntleroy, father of Catherine. Sur. and Wit.
John Fauntleroy. p. 85.

CORR, Braxton and Mary Hardy, of lawful age. Bond 2 December 1828. Sur.
and Wit. Robert Daniel, Robert Daniel, younger, and John Hardy. p.100.

CORR, Labon and Ann Montague. Bond 30 December 1814. Sur. and Wit. John
Owen. p.78.

CORR, Thomas and Polly Garret. Bond 29 December 1802. Henry Garret, deceased, father of Polly; Beverley Pierce, guardian. Sur. and Wit.
Beverley Pierce and Mary Garrett. p.55.

COULBOURN, William and Miss Henritta Berry. Married 26 May 1842 by Lewis
H. Williams. [Minister's return only.] p. 164.

COWLES, Edmund and Ann Wortham. Bond 24 December 1773. Sur. and Wit. James
Wortham and Machen Fearn. p.19.

CRAINE, William and Sarah Major Dillard. Bond 25 September 1786. Sur. and
Wit. James Clayton. p.30.

CREIGHTON, John R. and Miss Charlotte Jackson. Bond 16 January 1843.
Married 19 January 1843 by George Northam. Elizabeth Jackson, mother
of Charlotte. Sur. and Wit. James Norris and Thomas S. Harrow. p.122.

CRITCHER, George, of Richmond County, and Margaret M. Garrett. Bond 2 December 1846. Sur. and Wit. Edmund H. Montague and M. H. Groom. p.131.

CRITTENDEN, Robert and Miss Frances Mactyre. Bond 5 July 1845. Sur. and
Wit. Thomas Hundley and R. S. Mickelborough. p.128.

CRITTENDEN, Samuel S. and Catherine Hart. Bond 15 January 1850. Married
20 January 1850 by Zach Street. Elizabeth Seward, mother of Catherine.
Sur. and Wit. Lewis B. Seward and Sarah Key. p.138.

CRITTENDEN, Thomas and Jenny Kidd. Bond 23 January 1786. Sur. and Wit.
John Quarles. p.29.

CRITTENDEN, Thomas C. and (Jane) E. P. Beazley. Bond 16 December 1848.
Married 19 December 1848 by R. A. Christian. John H. Beazley, father
of Jane. Sur. and Wit. Robert H. Bray, Malvinas Beazley and John A.
Beazley. p.135.

CRITTENDEN, Zachariah and Catharine Jackson. Married 25 October 1804 by
Henry Heffernan. [Minister's return only.] p.155.

CRITTENDEN, Zachariah U. and Mrs. Martha A. Powers. Bond 25 March 1834.
Sur. and Wit. Holland Walker and Samuel Cole. p.114.

CROSSFIELD, James and Miss Nancy Alderson, in her 27th year. Bond 17 June 1807. John Thurston signs affidavit that Nancy's parents are dead and that she has been in his neighborhood ten or twelve years. Sur. and Wit. John Crossfield, John Thurston, and Elizabeth Thurston. p.64.

CROSSFIELD, John, widower, and Miss Polly Good. Bond 24 June 1809. John Good, father of Polly. Sur. and Wit. John Good. p.68.

CROSSFIELD, Leonard and Miss Charlotte Gulley, both 21 years. Bond 20 December 1810. Sur. James Crossfield. p.72.

CROSSFIELD, Samuel and Nancy Cooper, of lawful age. Bond 30 March 1830. Sur. and Wit. Ythel M. Parry, Thomas F. Taff, and John H. Parry. p.103.

CROUCH, Laurence and Miss Peggy Trice. Bond 28 January 1822. Thomas Trice, Sr., father of Peggy. Sur. and Wit. Thomas Trice, Sr. p.86.

CROXTON, John and Eunice D. McTyre. Bond 15 December 1817. Joseph McTyre, father of Eunice. Sur. and Wit. Lewis Walden and Mick^h Daniel. p.83.

CUNDIFF, Griffin and Mary Anderson, both of age. Bond 21 December 1808. Sur. and Wit. John A. Miles. p.67.

CUNDIFF, Griffin and Miss Ann Harrow. Bond 18 June 1823. William Harrow, father of Ann. Sur. and Wit. William Harrow. p.88.

CUNDIFF, Griffin and Mary Ann Berry. Bond 24 September 1851. Married 25 September 1851 by Holland Walker. Sur. and Wit. Josiah Ailworth. p.140.

CUNDIFF, William and Miss Permilia Blade, of age. Bond 21 February 1810. Sur. and Wit. John B. Long and John Layton, Sr. p.69.

CUNDIFF, William and Caty Boss. Bond 3 January 1815. Lewis Boss, father of Caty. Sur. and Wit. William Williams. p.78.

CURTIS, Charles and Anne Murray. Bond 20 December 1787. Married 22 December 1787 by Samuel Klug. Sur. and Wit. Cary Kemp, P. Blackburn, and Thomas Churchhill. p.32.

CURTIS, Robert C. and Miss Elizabeth Henry Fitzhugh. Bond 22 November 1833. Philip Fitzhugh, father of Elizabeth. Sur. and Wit. Francis (Frank) DuVal. p. 112.

CURTIS, William and Mary Robinson Whiting. Bond 24 May 1790. Married 5 June 1790 by Samuel Klug. Sur. and Wit. William Robinson and Machen Boswell. p.36.

CURTIS, William and Ariana Maria Grymes. Bond 1 February 1802. Married 6 February 1802 by Henry Heffernan. Philip L. Grymes, guardian of Ariana. Sur. and Wit. Charles Windham Grymes. p.54.

DALLAM, William J. and Miss Betty T. C. Muse. Bond 19 October 1831.
Married 20 October 1831 by George Northam. Elliott Muse, deceased,
father of Betty. Sur. and Wit. Thomas Muse. p.106.

DANCE, John and Ann Ross. Bond 29 May 1780. Sur. and Wit. Francis Ross.
p.23.

DANIEL, Carter and Elizabeth Kidd. Bond 27 January 1812. Burgess Kidd,
father of Elizabeth. Sur. and Wit. Burgess Kidd. p.73.

DANIEL, Elloson and Miss Addeline (Addy) L. Brooken (Brooking), of lawful
age. Bond 8 April 1828. Philip T. Montague, guardian of Adeline. Sur.
and Wit. Robert Daniel, Robert Daniel, Jr., and William Saddler. p.99.

DANIEL, Garrett and Polly Williams, above 21 years. Bond 11 February 1808.
Sur. and Wit. Beverly Daniel. p.66.

DANIEL, George and Mary Daniel. Bond 22 December 1752. Sur. and Wit. Henry
Daniel. p.7.

DANIEL, George and Miss Frances Daniel. Bond 9 September 1763. William
Daniel, Gent., deceased, father of Frances. Sur. and Wit. John Murray.
p.15.

DANIEL, George and Lucy Clare. Bond 10 February 1789. Married 12 February
1789 by Samuel Klug. Sur. and Wit. David Garland. p.34.

DANIEL, George B. and Miss Sarah W. Stiff, of age. Bond 26 December 1831.
Sur. and Wit. James W. Stiff and John R. Smith. p.107.

DANIEL, George B. and Ann Dudley. Married 11 January 1838 by George
Northam. [Minister's return only.] p.161.

DANIEL, George, Jr. and Miss Mary Jane Deagle. Bond 17 March 1845. Married
18 March 1845 by George Northam. Mary Deagle, mother of Mary. Sur. and
Wit. Josiah D. Ailworth and Lenox Ailworth. p.128.

DANIEL, James and Nancy Leaco. Bond 25 February 1793. Married 7 March 1793
by John Mullins. Sur. and Wit. John Daniel. p.40.

DANIEL, John, of age, and Miss Lucy Blake. Bond 9 November 1807. Married
9 December 1807 by David Corey. George Blake, father of Lucy. Sur.
and Wit. Spencer Clarke and Christopher Owen. p.65.

DANIEL, John W. and Matilda Sibley. Married 12 January 1837 by George
Northam. [Minister's return only.] p.160.

DANIEL, Lunsford and Lydia Daniel. Bond 2 July 1777. William Daniel, Sr.,
father of Lydia. Sur. and Wit. Nelson Daniel. p.21.

DANIEL, Mickelborough and Miss Elizabeth Garret. Bond 27 February 1823.
George Garret, father of Elizabeth. Sur. and Wit. George Garret. p.87.

DANIEL, Nelson and Jean Blackburn. Bond 3 February 1790. Married
6 February 1790 by Samuel Klug. Sur. and Wit. Benjamin Hackney. p.35.

DANIEL, Oliver and Mary Stevens, of age. Bond 29 December 1779. Sur. and
Wit. Daniel Jefferson. p.23.

DANIEL, Richard and Margret Gutery (Guthery), spinster. Bond 2 October
1764. Sur. and Wit. James Wortham. p.15.

DANIEL, Robert and Mrs. Lucy Daniel. Bond 9 January 1744. Sur. and Wit.
Robert Daniel, Thomas Price, and William Daniel. p.2.

DANIEL, Robert and Feby Sadler, over 21 years. Bond 26 November 1792. Sur.
and Wit. John Daniel. p.39.

DANIEL, Robert Jr. and Eliza Ware, under 21 years. Bond 24 March 1823.
Samuel Ware, father of Eliza. Sur. and Wit. Philip Montague and Erastus
T. Montague. p.87.

DANIEL, Vivion and Lucy Ann Daniel. Bond 23 November 1840. Mickelborough
Daniel, father of Lucy Ann. Sur. and Wit. Mickelborough Daniel. p.121.

DANIEL, William and Susannah George. Bond 14 September 1754. Sur. and Wit.
John George. p.8.

DANIEL, William H. and Martha A. Montague, over 21 years. Bond 14 March
1839. Robert Daniel, father of William, gives consent. Sur. and Wit.
Larkin D. Parry and Philip T. Montague. p. 118.

DARBY, John and Lucy Harrison Churchill. Bond 30 April 1793. Sur. and Wit.
Thomas Fauntleroy. p.40.

DARBY, John and Mrs. Lucy B. Churchill. Bond 14 December 1807. Married
15 December 1807 by Henry Heffernan. Lucy is widow of Thomas E.
Churchill. Sur. and Wit. Thomas Grymes. p.65.

DAVIS, Andrew, Jr. of Gloucester County, batchelor, and Lucia Staige,
spinster. Bond 1 March 1757. Sur. and Wit. William Young of Essex Co.,
and Robert Allcock. p.10.

DAVIS, Bartlett and Mrs. Ann Wood. Bond 27 November 1834. Sur. and Wit.
William Kellum. p.114.

DAVIS, Bartlett and Mrs. Lucy A. Matthews. Bond 23 May 1846. Married in
June 1846 by John J. Boss. Sur. and Wit. Josiah D. Ailworth and R. H.
Crittenden. p.130.

DAVIS, Currel and Miss Nancy Kellom. Bond 18 April 1812. Abel Kellom,
father of Nancy. Sur. and Wit. William Hill. p.74.

DAVIS, James and Elizabeth Humphries. Bond 21 December 1787. Married
28 January 1788 by Samuel Klug. Sur. and Wit. John Davis and William
Churchhill. p.32.

DAVIS, James and Miss Henrietta Fitzgerald. Bond 13 March 1822. Elijah
Fitzgerald, father of Henrietta. Sur. and Wit. Thomas Fitzgerald
[also shown Thomas F. Gerald.] p.86.

DAVIS, John Perkins and Susanna Boss. Married 29 October 1786 by John
Mullins. [Minister's return only.] p.146.

DAVIS, John P. and Miss Matilda Muire, of age. Bond 5 March 1828. Sur.
and Wit. George Muire. p.99.

DAVIS, Richard A. and Betsy Bushrod Walker. Bond 25 December 1826. Frank
Walker, father of Betsy. Sur. and Wit. Francis Walker. p.95.

DAVIS, Stapleton and Alice Blake. Married 23 November 1797 by Henry
Heffernan. [Minister's return only.] p.152.

DAVIS, William H. and Martha Ann Kidd. Bond 27 January 1840. Sur. and Wit.
Jacob Hart and Robert F. Stubbs. p.120.

DEAGLE, Absalom and Miss Nancy Renn Humphries, over 21. Bond 18 October 1806.
Sur. and Wit. William Norton, Jr. p.63.

DEAGLE, Ephraim and Miss Alice Woodley. Bond 8 June 1829. Married 8 June
1829 by George Northam. Abslum Deagle signs affidavit that Ephraim Deagle
is free from him. Sur. and Wit. Thomas Deagle and James Jackson. p.101.

DEAGLE, Ephraim (E.) and Miss Lucy Matthews. Bond 19 September 1834. Sur.
and Wit. Thomas Deagle and William M. Harrow. p.114.

DEAGLE, Ephraim E. and Pamela Trader. Bond 7 September 1852. Sur. and Wit.
R. H. Crittenden. p. 142.

DEAGLE, James and Lucy Davis, of age. Bond 24 October 1810. Sur. and Wit.
William Hill. p.71.

DEAGLE, James and Miss Sophia Layton, over 21 years. Bond 6 May 1826. Sur.
and Wit. Hiram Walker and Holland Walker. p.94.

DEAGLE, James and Miss Nancy Harrow, of lawful age. Bond 3 August 1830.
Married 5 August 1830 by George Northam. Sur. and Wit. George Trader and
James Jackson. p.104.

DEAGLE, John W. and Comfort Clayville. Bond 1 September 1851. Sur. and .
Wit. Thomas S. Hall. p.140.

DEAGLE, William and Miss Polly Kellom. Bond 18 April 1811. Absalom Deagle,
father of William. Abel Kellom, father of Polly. Sur. and Wit. William
Hill. p.74.

DEAGLE, William and Miss Rebecca Ann Trader. Bond 19 November 1833.
Absalom Deagle, father of William. Patsey Trader, mother of Rebecca.
Married 20 November 1833 by George Northam. Sur. and Wit. Ephraim
Deagle. p.112.

DEAGLE, William Henry and Mrs. Ann Hitchens. Married 22 September 1841
by Lewis H. Williams. [Minister's return only.] p.164.

DeBAPTISTE(BAPTIST), Benjamin (D.) and Nancy Woodford, over 21. Bond
3 January 1816. James Ross signs affidavit that Nancy was emancipated
14 July 1801. Sur. and Wit. Walter Healy. p.80.

DEAN, John and Frances Smith. Bond 16 September 1773. Consent of James
Mickelburrough. Sur. and Wit. William Dean, John Mitchell, and John
Dillard. p.18.

DENISON, Jonathan and Jane Morgan. Bond 13 December 1781. John Morgan,
deceased, father of Jane; Hugh Walker gives consent. Sur. and Wit.
Thomas Iverson and Thomas Montague. p.25.

DEW, William and Sarah Clarke. Bond 25 November 1776. Sur. and Wit.
Thomas Segar and Jasper Clayton. p.21.

DICKERSON, Eli and Judith Maderis. Bond 24 October 1796. Sur. and Wit.
Peter Taff. p.45.

DICKERSON, Henry and Miss Lucy P. Parry. Bond 15 December 1830. Sur. and
Wit. Robert Mackan, R. H. Street, and Benjamin Hundley. p.104.

DICKERSON, Henry and Miss Ailcy Maderris. Bond 6 June 1845. Sur. and Wit.
William H. Stone and John B. Dyke. p.128.

DICKERSON, Richard H. and Virginia S. Blackburn. Married 25 March 1841
by George Northam. [Minister's return only.] p.162.

DIDLAKE, Ammon and [Mary E. Wood]. Bond 20 December 1843. Married 21
December 1843 by George Northam. The name of the wife was omitted from
the marriage bond but was shown on the minister's return. "License
granted by verbal order of guardian, Didlake himself being guardian."
Sur. and Wit. Robert T. Mountain. p.124.

DIDLAKE, Philip and Alice Davis, above 21 years of age. Bond 5 February
1805. William Davis, deceased, father of Alice. Sur. and Wit. Bartley
Davis. p.60.

DIDLAKE, Robert and Frances Jesse. Bond 28 January 1829. John Jesse,
father of Frances. Sur. and Wit. James Gardner. p.100.

DIGGS, Dudley, Jr. of York County, and Elizabeth Wormeley. Bond 14 July
1760. Sur. and Wit. Thomas Price and Braxton Bird. p.12.

DILLARD, Edmund and Miss Catherine Lee. Bond 23 October 1817. Philip Lee,
deceased, father of Catherine. Sur. and Wit. Charles Lee. p.83.

DILLARD, Edmund L. and Elizabeth Daniel. Bond 28 July 1851. Married
28 July 1851 by Zach. Street. "Issued by consent of the father." Sur.
and Wit. Ellison Daniel. p.140.

DILLARD, George and Molly Batchelder. Bond 23 July 1792. Sur. and Wit. Benjamin Kidd, Jr. p.39.

DILLARD, William and Elizabeth Lamkin. Bond 9 August 1806. Elizabeth "was 21 years old on 4th of February last"; daughter of Milley Lamkin and sister of Fleet Lamkin. Sur. and Wit. Fleet Lamkin and Griffin McTuggle. p.62.

DIX, Thomas A. and Mrs. Mary Ann Wood. Bond 21 November 1843. Married 22 November 1843 by Richard A. Christian. Sur. and Wit. Alfred Healy, Richard H. Bristow, and M. B. Gressitt. p.123.

DOBSON, William and Eliza N. Blake. Bond 24 November 1824. Sur. and Wit. Samuel Blake and William Redwood. p.90.

DONAWAY, James and Martha Campbell (F.N.) both 21 years of age. Bond 9 March 1840. Married 10 March 1840 by Thomas B. Evans. Octavious Lawson of Lancaster County certifies that James Dunaway was free born. Sur. and Wit. John Sears. p.120

DRIVER, Richard and Elizabeth Taylor, widow. Bond 27 December 1803. Sur. and Wit. John Dean and John Woodley. p.57.

DRIVER, Richard and Elizabeth Bayley. Married 7 January 1804 by Argyle W. White. [Minister's return only. Apparently the same as above.] p.154.

DUDLEY, Charles and Nancy Sutton. Bond 25 August 1775. Rowland Sutton, father of Nancy. Sur. and Wit. Rowland Sutton. p.21.

DUDLEY, Charles and Miss Jane Kidd, over 21. Bond 9 December 1835. James Kidd, deceased, father of Jane. Sur. and Wit. John Brimm and Edmund H. Montague. p.116.

DUDLEY, George and Miss Precilla Miles. Bond 23 March 1820. William Miles, deceased, father of Precilla. Sur. and Wit. Jeremiah Jackson. p.84.

DUDLEY, John and Rachel Lee, age 21. Bond 26 December 1800. James Trice signs affidavit. Sur. and Wit. James Smith and Thomas Trice. p.52.

DUDLEY, John S. and Miss Milkey Ailworth. Bond 28 July 1827. Sur. and Wit. William Ailworth. p.97.

DUDLEY, Lewis and Frances Aldin. Bond 7 October 1761. Frances second daughter of John Aldin, deceased. Sur. and Wit. William Meacham, Ch^r Robinson, and Robert Elliot. p.12.

DUDLEY, Marlow and Anna Maria Ashton. Bond 23 February 1763. Sur. and Wit. William Moulson and Robert Elliot. p.14.

DUDLEY, Robert and Ann Blake. Bond 18 April 1789. Married 19 April 1789 by Samuel Klug. Sur. and Wit. Charles Dudley. p.34.

DUDLEY, Robert and Miss Elizabeth Norton. Bond 22 January 1837. Married 25 January 1837 by George Northam. Sur. and Wit. George D. Pace. p.116.

DUDLEY, Stanton, bachelor, and Miss Mary Berry, spinster. Bond 5 March 1760. Sur. and Wit. John Berry, William Segar, and George Daniel. p.11.

DUDLEY, Stanton and Judith Jackson. Bond 10 March 1796. Married 12 March 1796 by Henry Heffernan. Sur. and Wit. John B. Garland. p.44.

DUDLEY, Staunton and Miss Ann Blake. Bond 21 December 1832. Sur. and Wit. Warner C. Blake. p.110.

DUNAWAY, Presley and Judy Moulson. Bond 25 June 1792. Married 2 July 1792 by John Mullins. Sur. and Wit. William Kidd and Cary Kemp. p.38.

DUNGEE, Richard and Kittury Porter, free persons of color. Bond 14 January 1852. Married January 1851 by Thomas B. Evans. Jane Roberson, mother of Kittury. Sur. and Wit. Elijah Dungee, W. G. Daniel and M. Daniel. p.141.

DUNGEE, Thomas and Sarah Dungee. Bond 30 December 1844. Sur. and Wit. Anderson Jackson. p.127.

DUNLAVEY (DUNLEVEY), James W. and Mrs. Nancy Sibley. Bond 10 December 1816. Nancy is widow of John Sibley, deceased, and signs her own consent. Sur. Wit. William Beck. p.81.

DUNLAVEY, James and Frances E. Corr, of age. Bond 29 December 1830. Married 3 April 1831 by George U. Trice. Sur. and Wit. John H. Dunlavey. p.105.

DUNLAVEY, Robert W. and Polly Spann. Bond 14 November 1828. Married "between July 2, 1828 and July 2, 1829" by Nathan Healy. Thomas Spann, deceased, father of Polly. Sarah S. Spann signs affidavit that her daughter is 23 years of age. Sur. and Wit. Enos Healy and Edmund Healy. p.99.

DUNLAVY, John B. and Miss Catherine Robinson. Bond 10 January 1823. William Robinson, deceased, father of Catherine. Sur. and Wit. Isham Miller and Spencer Clark. p.87.

DUNLAVY, William B. and Mary Sadler (Mary E. Saddler.) Bond 26 November 1849. Married 18 December 1849 by Holland Walker. Sur. and Wit. James W. Dunlavy. p.137.

DUNLEVY, Braxton and Mary Hibble. Bond 20 December 1791. Sur. and Wit. William Healy. p.38.

DUNLEVY, George and Dorothy Wake. Bond 31 May 1800. Sur. and Wit. Pittman Wiatt. p.51.

DUNLEVY, John and Elizabeth Seward. Bond 25 November 1793. Married 25 December 1793 by John Mullins. Sur. and Wit. John Seward, Jr. and Thomas Iverson. p.41.

DUNN, Agrippa and Isabella Shipley, widow. Bond 22 April 1805. Sur. and Wit. Samuel Ware. p.60.

DUNN, Agrippa, widower, and Miss Elizabeth Lane, 21 years. Bond 3 December 1810. Sur. and Wit. James Quesenberry. p.71.

DUNN, Henry [or Harry] and Polly T. Seward. Bond 28 November 1811. Edward Seward, father of Polly. Sur. and Wit. Edward Seward. p.73.

DUNN, James and Catharine McTyre, above 21 years. Bond 15 January 1806. Ann Dunn of Essex County, guardian of James. Sur. and Wit. Thomas Ussery and William Parron. p.61.

DUNN, Peachy and Caty Leakes. Bond 2 January 1797. Sur. and Wit. James Daniel. p.46.

DUNN, Thomas and Polly McKan. Bond 25 June 1810. John McKan, deceased, father of Polly; John C. Warwick, her guardian. Sur. and Wit. John C. Warwick. p.70.

DYKE, William and Ann Beaman. Bond 26 January 1807. William Dyke, guardian of Ann. Sur. and Wit. Robert Dobbyns. p.63.

EASTHAM, William and Frances Bird. Bond 23 June 1753. R. Eastham, father of William. Sur. and Wit. William Young, John Shakelford, and Peter Bowmer. p.7.

EDWARDS, Charles and Sarah Sutton. Bond 22 October 1788. Married 24 October 1788 by Samuel Klug. Sur. and Wit. John Sutton. p.33.

EDWARDS, Thomas and Miss Lucy Ann J.B.Respess. Bond 3 February 1814. Henry Respess, deceased, father of Lucy; John Healy, guardian. Sur. and Wit. Richard M. Segar. p.77.

EGGLESTON, Joseph and Judith Segar. Bond 11 December 1753. Sur. and Wit. William Moulson and William Roane, Junior. p.8.

ELGAR, Philander and Lucy Bristow. Bond 7 May 1828. James B. Bristow, deceased, father of Lucy; Rebecca Robinson, guardian. Sur. and Wit. Enos Healy. p.97.

ELGAR, Samuel, above 21 years, and Dorothy Bray, above 21 years. Bond 30 December 1805. Sur. and Wit. James Healy. p.61.

ELLIOT, Robert and Miss Elizabeth Kemp, eldest daughter of Major Matthew Kemp, deceased. Bond 18 September 1742. Mary Kemp, guardian of her daughter. Sur. and Wit. Thomas Price, Luke Burford, and Lewis Montague. p.2.

ELLIOTT, Temple and Miss Roenna Greenwood. Bond 9 June 1843. Sur. and Wit. Thomas F. Taff. p.123.

ELLIOTT, William and Rebecca Deagle. Bond 3 May 1780. Sur. and Wit. Matthew Elliot. p.23.

ENOS, William H. of Gloucester County, and Mary Elizabeth Walker. Bond 5 June 1845. Married 5 June 1845 by George Northam. Joel Walker, father of Mary. Sur. and Wit. John T. West and Francis M. Walker. p.128.

EUBANK, James A. and Miss Cornelia E. Roane. Bond 19 December 1834. Lucy Roane, mother of Cornelia. Sur. and Wit. Braxton Clarke. p.115.

EVANS, Thomas B. and Miss Sarah E. Healy. Bond 7 November 1835. Married 12 November 1835 by George Northam. Walter Healy, father of Sarah. Sur. and Wit. Walter Healy. p.116.

EVANS, Thomas B. and Elizabeth Woodward. Married 19 October 1837 by George Northam. [Minister's return only.] p.161.

EVANS, Thomas R. Jr. and Miss Sarah S. Montague, of lawful age. Bond 17 January 1810. Thomas Montague, deceased, father of Sarah. Sur. and Wit. Thomas G. Crittenden and Christopher Owen. p.69.

FALKNER, John and Judith Fearn. Bond 20 November 1747. Sur. and Wit. William Owen and Richard Major. p.4.

FAULKNER, Richard C. and Miss Frances Lee. Bond 27 January 1812. Benjamin Faulkner, father of Richard. Charles Lee, Esq., deceased, father of Frances; Lewis Lee, her guardian. Sur. and Wit. Thomas F. Spencer, George C. New, and James Guthrey. p.73.

FAUNTLEROY, Samuel G. and Miss Lucy E. Cooke. Bond 2 January 1816. Thomas Cooke, deceased, father of Lucy. Sur. and Wit. Thomas Fauntleroy. p.80.

FAUNTLEROY, Samuel G. Jr. and Miss Elizabeth Pope Jones. Bond 24 September 1844. Sarah Jones, mother of Elizabeth. Sur. and Wit. John S. Healy, William T. Fauntleroy and William N. Walton. p.126.

FAUNTLEROY, Samuel G. Jr. of King and Queen County, and Fanny B. Claybrook. Bond 25 September 1848. Married 5 October 1848 by R. A. Christian. M.E. Claybrook, parent of Fanny. Sur. and Wit. William L. Claybrook and Z.L. Claybrook. p. 135.

FAUNTLEROY, Thomas and Isabella Lorimer. Bond 22 August 1796. Married 1 September 1796 by Henry Heffernan. Hannah T. Lorimer, mother of Isabella. Sur. and Wit. Christopher Harwood, John Montague, and Eleanor Craine. p.45.

FAUNTLEROY, Thomas W. and Miss Juliet M. Healy. Bond 29 December 1832. Walter Healy, father of Juliet. Sur. and Wit. John G. Smith. p.110.

FEARN, George and Mary Haslewood. Bond 1 September 1747. Sur. and Wit. John Rhodes, Junior, and Richard Major. p.4.

FEARN, George and Catherine Segar. Bond 4 September 1753. Sur. and Wit. Randolph Segar and William Segar. p.7.

FEARN, John and Mrs. Leanna Lee. Bond 31 December 1744. Sur. and Wit. Jacob Stiff. p.3.

FEARN, Thomas and Miss Martha Jones. Bond 12 August 1762. William Jones, father of Martha. Sur. and Wit. James Wortham, Elizabeth Elliot, Samuel Wortham, and Benjamin Douglas. p.13.

FEARN, Thomas and Miss Sarah Hackney. Bond 9 January 1767. Sur. and Wit. Benjamin Hackney. p.17.

FENNING, John, of age, and Miss Polly Long Blake. Bond 26 December 1808. Warner Blake, father of Polly. Sur. and Wit. Warner Blake. p.67.

FERNALD, George and Frances Madiex. Bond 21 June 1784. Sur. and Wit. Wilkinson Bayzey and Mary Barzey. p.27.

FIGG, John and Susanna Collier of Gloucester County. Married 30 March 1797 by Henry Heffernan, out of the county. [Minister's return only.] p.152.

FITZGERALD, Thomas and Mrs. Catherine Cundiff. Bond 10 September 1823. Catherine is widow of William Cundiff, deceased. Sur. and Wit. William M. Burke. p.88.

FITZHUGH, Patrick H. and Miss Mary S. Christian. Bond 2 November 1840. Married 10 November 1840 by George Northam. R. A. Christian, father of Mary. Sur. and Wit. Richard A. Christian. p.121.

FONTAINE, James Maury and Betty Carter Churchhill. Bond 31 December 1777. Sur. and Wit. John Jackson. p.21.

FOSTER, Major Samuel and Miss Nancy Chowning. Bond 11 September 1811. Ann A. Chowning gives consent. Sur. and Wit. Richard M. Segar, John Chowning, Jr., Lucy Shepherd, and Eunice B. Shepherd. p.72.

FRASER, Simon and Elizabeth Poythress, spinster. Bond 7 December 1775. Joshua Poythress, father of Elizabeth. Sur. and Wit. James Mills, Zach Shackelford, Thomas Fraser, Joshua Poythress, Jr., and William Poythress. p.21.

FRENCH, James and Miss Lucinda B. Clare. Bond 2 January 1824. Thomas Clare, deceased, father of Lucinda. Sur. and Wit. Robert Barrick. p.89.

FRENCH, William and Lucy Dunlevy. Bond 19 February 1796. Married 20 February 1796 by Henry Heffernan. Sur. and Wit. Braxton Dunlevy. p.44.

FRENCH, William T. and Amanda Dunlavy. Bond 26 November 1849. Married 6 December 1849 by Holland Walker. Sur. and Wit. James W. Dunlavy. p.137.

GAINES, Henry [or Harry] and Mirenda Muse [Mira on consent] Bond 9 March 1803. Thomas Muse, brother and guardian. Sur. and Wit. Peter Kemp,Jr., George Murray, and Charles Brooking. p.56.

GAINES, Thomas and Katy [Wortham.] Bond 16 April 1778. Katy's last name
not shown on bond, but written into marriage register. Charles Collins,
guardian of Thomas. Sur. and Wit. James Wortham. p.22.

GALLY, Foster P. and Mary Ann Dudley. Bond 27 August 1852. James Dudley,
father of Mary Ann. Sur. and Wit. W. B. Callis, James H. Callis, who
gives consent. p.142.

GAMES, John and Fanny Wood. Bond 30 December 1793. Married 2 January 1794
by John Mullins. Sur. and Wit. Samuel Wood and Norborne Berkeley. p.41.

GAMES, John T. and Mary Frances Bristow. Bond 19 November 1849. Married
in November 1849 by Thomas B. Evans. Sur. and Wit. John P. Bristow. p.137

GAMES, Thomas and Alice Wood. Bond 13 January 1794. Married 16 January
1794 by John Mullins. Sur. and Wit. William Wood. p.41.

GARDNER, Elliott and Miss Lucy Watts, above age of 21. Bond 19 December
1827. Sur. and Wit. Thomas Hundley, Jr. who swears to her age. p.98.

GARDNER, George, widower, and Miss Catharine Oliver. Bond 26 February 1810.
Francis Oliver, deceased, father of Catharine; Wilson Oliver, guardian.
Sur.and Wit. Wilson Oliver. p.69.

GARDNER, James and Miss Jenetta Davis. Bond 20 May 1829. Sur. and Wit.
Larkin Gardner. p.101.

GARDNER, Larkin and Ann Watts. Bond 28 January 1833. Sur. and Wit. John
Hardy. p.111.

GARDNER, Leroy and Judy Kidd. Bond 24 January 1849. Married January 1849
by Thomas B. Evans. Sur. and Wit. Enos Walden and John Walden. p.136.

GARDNER, Lewis and Matilda Oliver. Bond 5 June 1844. Sur. and Wit. Elliott
Gardner and John Gardner. p.126.

GARDNER, Reubin and Ann C. Gardner. Bond 1 January 1839. Sur. and Wit.
Larkin Gardner, George Gardner, and Lewis Gardner. p.118.

GARDNER, William and Miss Frances Wyatt, orphan. Bond 26 November 1821.
Sur. and Wit. Elijah Wyatt and Robert Lee, Jr. p.85.

GARLAND, John and Mary Wood. Bond 25 January 1799. Sur. and Wit. William
Wood. p.49.

GARLAND, John and Dalinda Thomas. Bond 8 January 1829. Married 15 January
1829 by George Northam. John Thomas, father of Dalinda. Sur. and Wit.
James U. Wood. p.100.

GARLAND, Robert and Sarah Barrick. Bond 13 March 1832. Robert Barrick,
father of Sarah. Sur. and Wit. John J. Crafton. p. 108.

GARRETT, Edward and Miss Mary E. Wake. Bond 12 December 1831. Married
15 December 1831 by George Northam. Sur. and Wit. Braxton Clarke and
Ann Wake. p.107.

GARRETT, Henry and Miss Mary E. McTyre. Bond 3 January 1844. Mary C.
McTyre, mother of Mary. Sur. and Wit. Mordecai B. Gressitt, Sarah J.
McTyre, and John Clare. p.125.

GARRETT, James and Elizabeth Seward. Bond 23 April 1798. Sur. and Wit.
Edward Seward and James Mill. p.48.

GARRETT, James and Frances Garrett. Bond 23 February 1830. Sur. and Wit.
George Garrett. p.103.

GARRETT, Lumpkin and Miss Frances S. Brown. Bond 24 May 1848. Married
25 May 1848 by R. A. Christian. Richard Garrett gives consent for
Lumpkin. Sur. and Wit. Smith W. Brown and Susan Brown. p.134.

GARRETT, Richard and Miss Nancy Taff, of age. Bond 1 February 1812.
Bartholomew Bristow signs affidavit as to Nancy's age. Sur. and Wit.
Thomas Bray. p.73.

GARRETT, Richard and Miss Frances C. Bristow. Bond 7 February 1845.
Married in February 1845 by Richard A. Christian. Sur. and Wit.
Thomas S. Bristow and Zach. W. Bristow. p.127.

GARRETT, Thomas H. and Elizabeth E. Seward. Bond 24 December 1838. Sur.
and Wit. Lewis Seward. p.118.

GATEWOOD, William L. and Lucy Ann Street. Bond 5 December 1833. Thomas
Street, Esq., father of Lucy. Sur. and Wit. Thomas Street. p.113.

GEORGE, John, Gent., and Elizabeth Alldin, widow. Bond 3 September 1765.
Sur. and Wit. Charles Lee. p.16.

GEORGE, John and Susanna George. Bond 11 May 1781. John George, father
of Susanna. Sur. and Wit. James Piggot. p.25.

GEORGE, Major John and Jane Meacham. Bond 26 March 1804. Married 29 March
1804 by Henry Heffernan. Sur. and Wit. P. Kemp, Jr., William Segar,
and Penelope Segar. p.58.

GEORGE, Leonard and Susanna George Daniel. Bond 28 December 1789.
Married 31 December 1789 by Samuel Klug. Sur. and Wit. Henry Daniel
Shepherd. p.35.

GEORGE, Leonard and Margaret Vance. Bond 29 July 1795. Married 6 August
1795 by Henry Heffernan. Sur. and Wit. John Brooks. p.43.

GEORGE, Thomas and Milly Kidd. Bond 3 December 1798. B. Kidd, Jr.,
father of Milly. Sur. and Wit. Thomas Kidd. p.49.

GEORGE, Captain William and Patty Jacobs, above 21 years. Bond 2 April
1804. Married 12 April 1804 by Henry Heffernan. Sur. and Wit. Robert
Blakey and B. Kidd. p.58.

GEORGE, William and Ann Batchelder (Bachelder.) Bond 29 March 1781.
Thomas Segar, guardian of Ann. Sur. and Wit. Charles Curtis, Robert
Thurston, and James Kidd. p.24.

GEORGE, William and Miss Joannah Lee. Bond 27 August 1827. Married
6 September 1827 by Richard Claybrook. Mildred Lee, mother of Joannah.
Sur. and Wit. Augustine Owen and Ann H. Lee. p.97.

GEORGE, William Jr. and Jane Warwick. Bond 22 April 1801. Sur. and Wit.
John Healy. p.52.

GEORGE, William Jr. and Elizabeth Greenwood, above 21 years. Bond 19 July
1804. Married 19 July 1804 by Henry Heffernan. Sur. and Wit.
Christopher Owen and Lewis Lee. p.59.

GIBSON, Charles and Nancy Mickleborough. Bond 11 January 1804. Married
13 January 1804 by Henry Heffernan. Sur. and Wit. Charles Robinson and
M. Daniel. p.59.

GIBSON, John and Polly Turner. Bond 26 October 1789. Sur. and Wit. John
Brooks. p.35.

GIBSON, John and Polly D. Didlake. Bond 12 September 1812. Thomas Ferguson,
father of Polly. Sur. and Wit. William Jesse and Philip Didlake. p.75.

GIBSON, John and Nancy J. Deagle. Bond 18 March 1839. Married 20 March
1839 by George Northam. William Deagle, father of Nancy. Sur. and Wit.
Archibald A. Taylor and William H. Deagle. p.118.

GIBSON, Wyatt and Sally Turner. Bond 28 November 1785. Married 23 December
1785 by Samuel Klug. Sur. and Wit. Henry Wyatt. p.28.

GILL, Alexander, bachelor, and Hannah Rice. Bond 17 April 1760. Sur. and
Wit. Robert Elliot. p.12.

GLEN, Matthew and Elizabeth Garland. Married 26 December 1797 by Henry
Heffernan. [Minister's return only.] p.152.

GODWIN, Joseph and Caty Price Shepherd. Bond 28 April 1806. John Seward,
guardian of Caty. Sur. and Wit. John Seward. p.62.

GODWIN, Richard and Miss Sarah Ann E. Jackson. Bond 1 April 1834. Married
5 April 1834 by Richard Claybrook. Richard Claybrook, guardian of Sarah.
Sur. and Wit. Robert McKan. p.114.

GOLEMAN, Willis and Sally Meggs. Bond 11 January 1820. James Meggs, father
of Sally. Sur. and Wit. Robert Meggs. p.84.

GOOD, James and Sarah South. Bond 24 May 1796. Sur. and Wit. Bartholomew
Bristow. p.45.

GOOD, Madison and Mrs. Maria G. Noel. Bond 14 June 1843. Sur. and Wit.
William N. Walker, William L. Gatewood, and John Gardner. p. 123.

GOOD, William N. and Nancy Seward. Bond 12 December 1848. Married 13 December 1848 by R. A. Christian. Sur. and Wit. Henry Sears and John Walden, Jr. p.135.

GOODE, James and Mrs. Polly South. Bond 28 October 1823. Polly is the widow of John South, deceased. James Goode swears that Polly South is no relation to him in anyway. Sur. and Wit. Enos Healy. p.88.

GOODE, John,Jr. and Miss Nancy Garrett, both over 21 years. Bond 22 June 1812. Sur. and Wit. Dabney A. Miller, John Owen, Thomas Goode and Harry Thurston. p.74.

GOODE, John and Mrs. Lucy Dudley. Bond 29 July 1828. Sur. and Wit. Henry T. Wyatt and Martha Wyatt. p.99.

GOODE, John S. and Mary Lewis. Bond 13 January 1830. Sur. and Wit. William Lewis. p.102.

GOODE, Thomas and Mrs. Elizabeth Dunn. Bond 18 August 1814. Elizabeth Dunn is widow of Agrippa Dunn, deceased. Sur. and Wit. John Faucett. p.77.

GOODE, William and Elizabeth Abbott. Bond 13 October 1788. Married 30 October 1788 by James Greenwood. Sur. and Wit. Nicholas Tuggle. p.33.

GOOLRICK, James and Mrs. Emily D. Hord. Bond 15 October 1827. Married 15 October 1827 by Richard Claybrook. Sur. and Wit. R. A. Christian. p.98.

GORDON, James of Lancaster County, and Mary Harrison. Bond 10 November 1748. Sur. and Wit. William Churchhill and Richard Major. p.4.

GORDON, John and Lucy Churchill, spinster. Bond 16 December 1756. A. Churchhill gives consent. Sur. and Wit. John Churchhill, Robert Elliott, and William Moulson. p.9.

GRAVES, Lewis and Rosa A. Taylor. Married 31 December 1849 by Holland Walker. [Minister's return only.] p.168.

GREENWOOD, Thomas and Elizabeth Howard. Married 24 December 1835 by George Northam. [Minister's return only.] p.160.

GREENWOOD, William C. and Miss Elizabeth Gerauld (Gerald). Bond 8 November 1830. Married 24 November 1830 by George Northam. Sur. and Wit. William L. Norton. p.104.

GRESHAM, Richard T. A., of Richmond County, and Lucy Ann Bristow. Bond 13 August 1850. Married 14 August 1850 by R. A. Christian. Sur. and Wit. Lewis S. Bristow. p.139.

GRESSITT, John D. and Virginia E. Muse. Bond 18 May 1852. Married 18 May 1852 by R.A.Christian. Ann Muse, mother of Virginia. Sur. and Wit. John E. Segar. p.142.

GRESSITT, Mordecai B. and Mary S. Muse. Bond 22 March 1843. Married
22 March 1843 by R. A. Christian. Ann Muse, mother of Mary, and also
her guardian. Sur. and Wit. R. A. Christian, Jr. and B. F. Cauthorn.
p.123.

GROOM, John and Catharine [Ware]. Bond 24 May 1779. Catharine's last
name was not given on bond, but was written into marriage register.
Sur. and Wit. George Saunders. p.22.

GROOM, Zachariah and Elizabeth Wyett. Bond 25 May 1789. Married 28 May
1789 by Samuel Klug. Sur. and Wit. Thomas Saunders, William Wyett,
Thomas Lambuth, and John Groom. p.34.

GROOME, Thomas and Mrs. Elizabeth Kidd. Bond 18 July 1830. Married 22 July
1830 by Richard Claybrook. Sur. and Wit. William Pittman. p.104.

GRYMES, Benjamin and Sarah Robinson. Bond 8 October 1773. Peter Robinson,
deceased, father of Sarah; John Robinson, her guardian. Sur. and Wit.
Thomas Digges, Benjamin Churchhill, and C. Armistead. p.18.

GRYMES, Philip Ludwell and [Judith Wormeley.] Bond 29 May 1773. The wife's
name does not appear on bond, but it is written into marriage register.
Sur. and Wit. Benjamin Grymes, Jr., and Will Churchhill. p.18.

GRYMES, Philip, Jr. and Sarah Robinson Steptoe. Bond 19 May 1804. Married
20 May 1804 by Henry Heffernan. Elizabeth Steptoe, mother of Sarah.
Sur. and Wit. Randolph Wormeley, Therit Towles, and Thomas Steptoe. p.58.

GULLEY, Philip and Mary Sutton. Bond 9 November 1782. Sur. and Wit.
Thomas Healy and John Crandall. p.26.

GUNDREY, John and Nancy Bennet. Bond 14 December 1824. Sur. and Wit. John
Brown. p.90.

GWATHMEY, Richard and Charlotte Spratt. Bond 24 May 1784. Sur. and Wit.
Overton Cosby. p.27.

HACKNEY, Benjamin and Mary Stiff. Bond 3 April 1782. Sur. and Wit. William
Stiff. p.25.

HACKNEY, Benjamin and Jane George. Bond 23 May 1785. Sur. and Wit. John
George. p.28

HACKNEY, James Henry and Mrs. Mary A. Healy. Married 12 October 1842 by
Richard A. Christian. [Minister's return only.] p.166.

HAGGOMAN, John and Miss Sarah Terrier. Bond 29 November 1826. John
Terrier, deceased, father of Sarah; W. Bohannon, her guardian. Sur. and
Wit. Thomas Terrier and Elijah Barnum. p.95.

HAILE, John Jr. and Miss Elizabeth Jackson. Bond 26 October 1812. William Jackson, deceased, father of Elizabeth; Martha Jackson, her guardian. Sur. and Wit. Dabney A. Miller and James Healy. p.75.

HAILE, Joseph and Miss Elizabeth H. Dunlevy. Bond 20 February 1832. Sur. and Wit. Iverson Charles. p. 107.

HAILE, Joseph and Mrs. Julia McKan. Bond 21 March 1848. Sur. and Wit. Ira E. Parry. p.133.

HAILE, Thomas and Frances Oliver, of age. Bond 7 June 1825. Sur. and Wit. John Haile. p.92.

HAILE, William H. and Miss Lucy Ann Wood. Bond 13 November 1846. Married 14 November 1846 by George Northam. Andrew Stiff, guardian of Lucy. Sur. and Wit. Ammon Didlake and Elizabeth Stiff. p.131.

HALL, Addison (Colonel) and Miss Catharine C. Crittenden. Bond 17 July 1832. Sur. and Wit. Zach. W. Crittenden. p.109.

HALL, Charles and Miss Penelope Walton. Bond 27 June 1825. Sur. and Wit. James R. Steptoe. p.92.

HALL, Gideon, over 21, and Anna Catharine Revere, over 21 years. Bond 3 December 1838. Married 6 December 1838 by George Northam. Sur. and Wit. Lawson Reveer. p.117.

HALL, Nathan and Catharine Crossfield. Bond 25 January 1790. Married 28 January 1790 by Samuel Klug. Sur. and Wit. Thomas Hall. p.35.

HALL, Thomas and Miss Jane Sears. Bond 10 January 1833. Sur. and Wit. Corrie Lee. p.111.

HALL, Thomas S. and Pelina J. Carter. Bond 4 December 1849. Married in December 1849 by R. A. Christian. Emily P.S.P.Carter, mother of Pelina. Sur. and Wit. Hiram Carter. p.137.

HALL, William and Miss Martha Clare [Miss Martha Hall on bond.] Bond 27 April 1835. C. Braxton, guardian of Martha. Sur. and Wit. George W. Barrick. p.116.

HARDEE, Curtis and Mary Carter, widow. Bond 23 November 1745. Sur. and Wit. Thomas Berry and Luke Burford. p.3.

HARDEE, John of Gloucester County, and Michal Sutton. Bond 7 March 1752. Michal was born 11 January 1728, and is the daughter of Christopher and Hope Sutton. Sur. and Wit. William Segar. p.6.

HARDEE, John and Mary Daniel. Bond 4 March 1789. Married 6 March 1789 by John Mullins. Sur. and Wit. Thomas Brooks. p.34.

HARDEE, William and Mary Meaderas. Bond 13 January 1795. Married
21 January 1795 by Robert Ware. Sur. and Wit. Thomas Brooks. p.42.

HARDIN, Thomas and Lucy Billups. Bond 5 January 1747. Sur. and Wit.
John Rhodes, Jr. and Richard Major. p.4.

HARDY, John and Miss Mary Harper. Bond 28 November 1831. Sur. and
Wit. Edward Seward and Edward S. Seward. p.106.

HARDY, Joseph and Jean Williams. Bond 22 January 1798. Sur. and Wit.
Reuben Lee and Thomas Kemp. p.48.

HARDY, William and Hannah Cornelius, who is 21. Bond 10 February 1802.
Sur. and Wit. William Parron. p.54.

HARRIS, Thomas of King and Queen County, and Betsy Key. Bond 17 December 1849. Thomas Key, father of Betsy. Sur. and Wit. Joseph
Key, William L. Gatewood, and William K. Gatewood. p.137.

HARROW, John and Miss Nancy Woodley. Bond 8 October 1821. Thomas
Woodley, deceased, father of Nancy. Sur. and Wit. John Brown. p.85.

HARROW, Martin O. and Elizabeth Vaughan. Married 26 January 1807.
[Listed with Minister's returns, but no minister's name given.] p.156.

HARROW, William and Jane [or Jean] Miles. Bond 30 December 1801.
William Miles, father of Jane. Sur. and Wit. William Wake. p.53.

HARROW, William and Miss Mary Frances Anderton. Married 29 July 1841
by Lewis H. Williams. [Minister's return only.] p.164.

HARROW, William M. and Miss Mary Almedia Carter. Bond 23 February 1835.
Married 25 February 1835 by George Northam. Hiram Carter gives
consent for Mary. Sur. and Wit. William K. Pace. p.115.

HART, John and Miss Mary A. Prichett. Bond 24 September 1827. Sur.
and Wit. William S. Berry and Thomas J. Berry. p.98.

HART, Richard H. and Miss Salley Montgomery, above the age of 21. Bond
8 November 1830. Married 10 November 1830 by George Northam. Nancy
Montgomery, mother of Salley. Sur. and Wit. Henry Wroten. p.104.

HART, Selby and Eliza A. Ailworth. Married 17 July 1831 by George
Northam. [Minister's return only. See Sibly Heart page 40.] p.159.

HARWOOD, Christopher and Eleanor Craine. Bond 23 August 1796. Married
1 September 1796 by Henry Heffernan. John and Sarah Maria Craine,
parents of Eleanor, who was born 7 April 1775. Sur. and Wit. Thomas
T. Montague and Foxhall Sturman. p.43.

HARWOOD, Thomas and Lucy Meacham. Bond 24 August 1778. Sur. and Wit.
John George. p.22.

HARWOOD, William Chichester Curtis and Miss Hannah U. Wood. Bond
19 December 1822. Tholemiah Wood, deceased, father of Hannah;
John Chowning, Jr., her guardian. Sur. and Wit. John Chowning, Jr.,
Charles C. Willford, Ph. C. Rowe, and G. A. Jones. p.86.

HAYNIE, Holland and Myra Webb. Bond 17 September 1781. Sur. and Wit.
James Montague. p.25.

HAYWOOD, William and Lucy Risby. Bond 5 December 1848. Married 5 December 1848 by Holland Walker. Sur. and Wit. Henry L. Mathews and
M. W. Haile. p.135.

HEALY, Alfred and Juliett E. Owen. Bond 31 December 1835. Married by
George Northam. [Minister's return only.] p.160.

HEALY, Alfred and Mary Jane Chowning. Bond 20 May 1839. Married 23 May
1839 by George Northam. Sur. and Wit. George T. R. Healy, E. D. Street,
and Thomas Street. p.118.

HEALY, Edmund and Miss Mary New. Bond 9 November 1813. James New,
deceased, father of Mary. Sur. and Wit. Robert Wooddy. p.76.

HEALY, Enos and Miss Elizabeth Seward. Bond 27 August 1829. Sur. and
Wit. Edward Seward. p.102.

HEALY, Enons and Ann H. Bray. Married 26 January 1821 by John Spencer.
p.156. [This is recorded in the marriage register, but the original
bond and minister's return are missing.] p.156.

HEALY, George and Harriott Roane. Bond 20 December 1809. Colonel
Thomas Roane, deceased, father of Harriott; Thomas Muse, her guardian.
Sur. and Wit. Thomas Muse and Henry Muse. p.68.

HEALY, George and Mrs. Martha G. Stamper. Bond 27 October 1830.
Married 3 November 1830 by George Northam. Sur. and Wit. R. A.
Christian and Richard Allen Christian. p.104.

HEALY, James, Jr. and Elizabeth M. Jones. Married 18 October 1804 by
Henry Heffernan. [Minister's return only.] p.155.

HEALY, James T. and Miss Mary Frances Fogg, 21 years of age. Bond
13 December 1848. Married in December 1848 by Thomas B. Evans. Sur.
and Wit. James Keiningham and Robert H. Bray. p.135.

HEALY, John S. and Betty T. C. Dallam. Married 3 February 1842 by
Richard A. Christian. [Minister's return only.] p.166.

HEALY, Nathan and Miss Mary Ann Bristow. Bond 11 December 1822.
Leanard Bristow, deceased, father of Mary Ann; Richard Segar, her
guardian. Sur. and Wit. Richard M. Segar. p.86.

HEALY, Robert and Miss Arreanna M. Owen. Bond 8 March 1826. C. Owen,
deceased, parent of Arreanna. Sur. and Wit. Thomas Street. p.94.

HEALY, Thomas and Sarah Mitchell. Bond 11 October 1785. Married
29 October 1785 by Samuel Klug. Sur. and Wit. Robert Stamper. p.28.

HEALY, Thomas Jr. and Frances Montague. Bond 28 April 1797. Married
6 May 1797 by Henry Heffernan. Sur. and Wit. Gabriel Jones. p.46.

HEALY, Thomas L. and Miss Jenetta Elgar. Bond 10 January 1833. Sur.
and Wit. Robert Bray, Dorothy Elgar, and James N. Henly. p.111.

HEALY, Walter and Miss Juliet T. Corbin. Bond 5 November 1815. John
T. Corbin, deceased, father of Juliet. Sur. and Wit. Elliott Muse
and George W. Banks. p.79.

HEALY, William and Elizabeth Bristow. Bond 20 December 1791. Sur. and
Wit. Braxton Dunlevy. p.38.

HEARN, John and Mrs. Elizabeth Anderton, widow. Bond 15 August 1831.
Married 27 August 1831 by George Northam. Sur. and Wit. William
Norton, William Ailworth, and Josiah Ailworth. p.106.

HEART (HARTE), Sibly [also shown Silbey] and Miss Eliza Ann Ailworth.
Bond 15 July 1831. William Ailworth gives consent for Eliza. Sur. and
Wit. Henry Muse, Jr. and Josiah Ailworth. [See Selby Hart page 38.] p.106.

HEFFERNAN, Rev. Henry and Lucy Nelson Berkeley. Bond 18 September 1800.
Edmund Berkeley, father of Lucy. Sur. and Wit. Peter Kemp, Jr. p.51.

HENING, Lewis and Jane Chapman, of lawful age. Bond 20 October 1791.
Sur. and Wit. John Daniel and John Montague. p.37.

HIBBLE, John and Elizabeth Haynes. Married 17 January 1789 by Samuel
Klug. [Minister's return only.] p.148.

HIBBLE, John and Mary French. Bond 22 August 1789. Married 25 August
1789 by Samuel Klug. Sur. and Wit. William Robinson and Peter Robinson.
p.34.

HILL, John and Nancy Scott. Bond 23 May 1794. Sur. and Wit. John
Sutton. p.42.

HILL, John P. and Elizabeth Watts. Bond 2 February 1829. Sur. and Wit.
Leroy H. Trice. p.100.

HILL, Leonard and Miss Sarah Thacker. Bond 4 October 1752. Sur. and
Wit. Lewis Burwell. p.6.

HILL, Needles and Miss Letitia Morgan. Bond 4 October 1758. Sur. and
Wit. Ph. Mountague. p.10.

HILL, William and Sarah Blake. Bond 22 September 1787. Married 23
September 1787 by John Mullins. p.31.

HILL, William and Nancy Davis. Bond 1 February 1804. Married
6 February 1804 by William Fritchett of Mathews County. Sur.
and Wit. William Norton and William Matthews. p.57.

HODGES, John and Elizabeth Blackburn. Bond 24 October 1785. Married
3 December 1785 by Samuel Klug. Sur. and Wit. Edmund Berkeley. p.28.

HOLLINS, William and Ann Hundley. Married 21 June 1845 by John J.
Boss. [Minister's return only.] p.167.

HOLT, William and Polly Fisher. Bond 28 July 1791. Sur. and Wit.
Thomas Clare. p.37.

HOPKINS, James and Jane Gibson. Bond 23 May 1786. Mary Hopkins,
mother of Jane, gives consent. Sur. and Wit. James Stiff and
Jonathan Lyell. p.30.

HOPKINS, James and Sarah Brooks. Bond 14 April 1792. Sur. and Wit.
John Woods. p.38.

HOPKINS, James and Susannah Davis. Bond 10 November 1803. Sur. and
Wit. John B. Garland, Joseph Moss and Elsebeth Moss. p.57.

HOPKINS, Richard,Jr. and _____ _____ [name omitted.] Bond 2 May 1764.
Sur. and Wit. James Gibson and James Wortham. p.15.

HOPKINS, Richard and Frances Blake. Bond 22 December 1786. Married
26 December 1786 by Samuel Klug. Mary Hopkins, mother of Richard,
gives consent. Sur. and Wit. John Blake. p.30.

HORSELY, Dudley and Miss Lucy South. Bond 1 December 1845. Married
1 December 1845 by Richard A. Christian. Mary H. South, mother
of Lucy. Sur. and Wit. Thomas Jones and Hugh D. South. p.129.

HOWARD, Allen and Elizabeth Mickelburrough. Bond 27 March 1787. Married
12 May 1787 by Samuel Klug. Sur. and Wit. Thomas Healy. p.31.

HOWARD, Allen and _____ _____[name omitted.] Bond 28 September 1807.
Sur. and Wit. Henry Mickelborrough. p.65.

HOWARD, Allen,Jr. and Frances Blackley, both of age. Bond 24 June 1814.
Sur. and Wit. Capt. Meachum Owen. p.77.

HOWARD, Lewis and Miss Sarah Trader. Bond 22 January 1833. Martha
Trader, mother of Sarah. Sur. and Wit. Richard Towell. p.111.

HOWERTON, Henry and Miss Elizabeth Daniel. Bond 18 April 1812. John
Daniel, father of Elizabeth. Sur. and Wit. John J. Willis. p.74.

HOWLAND, William and Miss Ann Hundley. Bond 23 June 1845. Sur. and
Wit. George W. Daniel and Thomas G. Hundley. p.128.

HUDGIN, William and Miss Ann Blake. Bond 21 August 1809. James Blake, deceased, father of Ann. Sur. and Wit. Thomas Healy, Jr. p.68.

HUDGINGS, William and Mildred Brown. Bond 25 August 1852. Sur. and Wit. R. T. Mountain. p.142.

HUGHES, John W. and Miss Julia Ann Clayton. Bond 25 November 1839. Married 5 December 1839 by George Northam. John Hughes of Gloucester County, father of John. Julia Ann was 21 years old on 17 September 1838. Sur. and Wit. No signatures. p.119.

HUMPHRIES, John and Priscilla Stevens. Bond 9 July 1804. Married 9 July 1804 by William Fritchett of Mathews County. Sur. and Wit. Edward Fordham and P. Kemp. p.58.

HUMPHRIES, John and Miss Margaret S. Mickelborough, above the age of 21. Bond 16 December 1828. Sur. and Wit. Thomas Hundley, Jr. p.100.

HUMPHRIES, Staige and Diana Barrock. Bond 7 December 1801. Married 12 December 1801 by Henry Heffernan. Seaton Humphries, guardian of Staige. David Barrock, father of Diana. Sur. and Wit. Seaton Humphries and John Barrock. p.53.

HUMPHRIES, William and Elizabeth Davis, widow. Bond 27 February 1800. Married 2 March 1800 by Henry Heffernan. John Humphries, father of William. Sur. and Wit. John Humphries and John Chew, Jr. p.51.

HUMPHRIES, William C. and Elizabeth Wiatt. Married 14 November 1799 by Henry Heffernan. [Minister's return only.] p.153.

HUMPHRIS, Nelson and Lucy Jones. Bond 10 April 1792. Sur. and Wit. John Humphries, Jr. p.38.

HUNDLEY, Lewis and Frances Dunn. Bond 22 December 1823. Peachy Dunn, parent of Frances. Sur. and Wit. William Stewart and John Downly. p.88.

HUNDLEY, Thomas,Sr. and Miss Harriet Maderis. Bond 11 February 1823. James Maderis, deceased, father of Harriet. Sur. and Wit. George M. Hundley and Henry Maderis. p.87.

HUNDLEY, Thomas and Miss Elizabeth A. Daniel. Bond 19 June 1845. Married 20 June 1845 by John J. Boss. Elizabeth Daniel, mother of Elizabeth. Sur. and Wit. George W. Daniel. p.128.

HUNLEY, Thomas and Miss Julia Mickelborough. Bond 15 January 1816. Sur. and Wit. Henry Mickelborough. p.80.

HUNLY, John and Miss Nancy Moore. Bond 2 June 1845. Job Moore, father of Nancy. Sur. and Wit. William Green. p.128.

HUNTINGTON, Adoniram Judson and Miss Elizabeth G. Christian. Bond 5 June 1844. Married 6 June 1844 by George Northam. Sur. and Wit. Richard A. Christian. p.126.

ISAAC, Fisher and Nancy Mullins. Bond 11 March 1815. Reuben Cauthorn of Essex County, guardian of Isaac. Nancy Mullins gives consent for Nancy. Sur. and Wit. Thomas Greenwood, John Cauthorn and Mary G. Mullins. p.79.

IVERSON, Thomas of Gloucester County, bachelor, and Jane Mountague, spinster. Bond 23 December 1757. Vincent Vass gives consent for Jane. Sur. and Wit. Robert Elliot, William Moulson, Jn. Psinstsoff, Phi. Mountague, and John Davis. p.10.

IVESON, Richard of Gloucester County, and Rebecca Dudley. Bond 12 February 1762. Rebecca is widow of William Dudley, deceased. Sur. and Wit. Robert Johnston and William Bickham. p.13.

IVY, Thomas and Anne Dudley. Bond 4 December 1751. Sur. and Wit. Christopher Curtis. p.6.

JACKSON, George and Fanny Campbell. Bond 17 December 1793. Sur. and Wit. Dudley Vaughan. p.41

JACKSON, James and Frances Read. Bond 26 November 1805. Francis Read, father of Frances. Sur. and Wit. William Wake and John B. Mountain. p.60.

JACKSON, James Henry, age 30 years, widower and Anner Hudgins Boss, age 23 years, single. Married 10 October 1853 by Holland Walker at Edward Garrett's. John M. and Rebecca Jackson, parents of James, who was born in Accomac County. John J. and Ann Boss, parents of Anner, who was born in Middlesex County. [Minister's return only.] p.170.

JACKSON, James R. and Jisey Kellum. Bond 7 October 1833. Nancy Kellum, mother of Jisey. Sur. and Wit. J. L. Jackson. p.112.

JACKSON, Jeremiah and Miss Betsey Miles. Bond 21 July 1809. William Miles, father of Betsey. Sur. and Wit. Griffin Cundiff and William Wake. p.68.

JACKSON, Jeremiah B. and Amanda Gladen. Married 25 January 1838 by George Northam. [Minister's return only.] p.161.

JACKSON, John and Sarah Blake. Bond 7 October 1755. John Blake, "late of this county," father of Sarah. Sur. and Wit. Robert Daniel, Jr. and James Webb, Jr. p.9.

JACKSON,John,Jr. and Mary Smith. Bond 7 March 1783. Sur. and Wit. John Smith. p.27.

JACKSON, John,Jr. and Catharine Davis. Bond 28 February 1785. Sur. and Wit. Adam Aldridge. p.28.

JACKSON, John L., of age, and Lucy Kellum. Bond 17 April 1826. Nancy Kellum, mother of Lucy. James Jackson gives affidavit as to John's age. Sur. and Wit. William Kellum. p.94.

JACKSON, John L. and Mrs. Ann Hart. Bond 28 April 1845. Married
29 April 1845 by George Northam. Sur. and Wit. Josiah D.
Ailworth and Lenox Ailworth. p.128.

JACKSON, Leonard and Miss Nancy Taylor Mickelborough. Bond 21 December 1814. Sur. and Wit. James Crittenden. p.78.

JACKSON, Richard and Mrs. Sarah Miles. Bond 1 November 1814. Sarah
is widow of John A. Miles, deceased. Sur. and Wit. James Jackson.
p.78.

JACKSON, Samuel Richard, age 28 years, widower, and Mary Elizabeth Ann
Towill, 16 years, single. Married 23 February 1854 by Holland Walker
at Mark W. Towill's. John M. and Rebecca Jackson, parents of Samuel,
who was born in Accomac County. Mark W. and Elizabeth Towill, parents
of Mary. [Minister's return only.] p.171.

JACKSON, William and Martha Vaughan. Bond 21 January 1791. Sur. and
Wit. Dudley Vaughan. p.36.

JACKSON, William and Martha Vass. Bond 7 May 1792. Sur. and Wit.
Thomas Montague and Thomas Churchill. p.38.

JAMES, William and Susanna Minter. Bond 9 January 1802. John Minter,
father of Susanna. Sur. and Wit. John B. Garland. p.54.

JAMES, William and Elizabeth Major. Bond 20 December 1787. Married
22 December 1787 by .Samuel Klug. Sur. and Wit. David Garland and
Thomas Churchhill. p.32.

JARVIS, John and Mary Dame. Bond 24 October 1796. Married 11 November
1796 by Henry Heffernan. Sur. and Wit. George Dame. p.45.

JEFFERSON, Daniel and Priscilla Barrick. Bond 30 July 1779. Sur. and
Wit. Benjamin Barrick. p.23.

JEFFERSON, John and Miss Nancy Dunlavy. Bond 13 June 1809. James
Dunlevy, deceased, father of Nancy. Braxton Dunlevy signs affidavit
that Nancy is 23 years of age. Sur. and Wit. James S. Standard and
Thomas M. Lock. p.68.

JEFFERSON. Rev. John and Elizabeth Burton, of lawful age. Bond
14 December 1824. Mary Burton, mother of Elizabeth. Sur. and Wit.
Meacham C. Boss and James Harrow. p.90.

JESSE, John and Elizabeth Street. Bond 26 February 1787. Married
8 March 1787 by William Mullins. Sur. and Wit. Lawrence Meacham.
p.31.

JESSE, John A. and Bettie C. Hoskins. Bond 12 February 1849. Sur. and
Wit. N. C. Montague. p.136.

JESSE, Richard and Frances Chowning. Bond 12 October 1793. Married
13 October 1793 by John Mullins. Sur. and Wit. Robert Chowning. p.41.

JESSE, Thomas, Jr. and Caty Ware. Bond 1 January 1805. Sur. and Wit.
John Jesse, Jr., John Seward, and William Jesse. p.59.

JESSE, Thomas and Elizabeth Shackelford. Bond 22 December 1828. Sur.
and Wit. Richard Claybrook. p.100.

JESSE, William T., Esq. of Lancaster County, and Miss Mary D. Claybrooke.
Bond 27 December 1837. Married 28 December 1837 by George Northam.
George Wright, guardian of Mary. Sur. and Wit. Augustine Owen, Ed-
ward L. Wright, and R. A. Claybrook. p.117.

JESSEE, John, Jr. and Polly Trice. Bond 21 May 1798. John Jessee,
guardian of John. James Trice, father of Polly. Sur. and Wit. John
Seward and Churchhill Blackburn. p.48.

JOHNSON, John and Miss Martha J. Clarke. Bond 22 November 1833. John
Clark, father of Martha. Sur. and Wit. William D. Clarke and John
Street. p.113.

JOHNSON, John L. and Louisa Bland. Bond 11 November 1850. Archer
Bland gives consent. Sur. and Wit. Lewis S. Bristow. p.139.

JOHNSON, Thomas M. and Miss Henthia Humphries. Bond 23 September 1815.
Seaton Humphries, deceased, father of Henthia. Sur. and Wit. George
Healy and Thomas M. Johnson. p.79.

JONES, Charles and Hannah Blackburn, spinster. Bond 27 August 1743.
Sur. and Wit. John Price and James Hodges. p.2.

JONES, Churchill and Melicent Blackburne. Bond 23 February 1744.
Elizabeth Blackburn, mother of Melicent. Sur. and Wit. Robert
Elliott, Lewis Montague, Hannah Jones, and Edward Blackburn. p.2.

JONES, Churchill and Ann Kemp. Bond 24 May 1756. Sur. and Wit.
Robert Elliott and Curtis Hardee. p.9.

JONES, Gabriel and Elizabeth Healy. Bond 11 December 1792. Sur. and
Wit. John N. Hill. p.39.

JONES, Isaac and Miss Betsey Owen. Bond 1 June 1811. John Owen,
deceased, father of Betsey Owen. Sur. and Wit. Henry Heffernan.
p.72.

JONES, Lewis and Sally Robinson. Bond 28 May 1827. William Robinson,
father of Sally. Sur. and Wit. William Robinson. p.97.

JONES, Thomas and Miss Elvira Robinson. Bond 8 January 1827. William
Robinson, father of Elvira. Sur. and Wit. William Robinson. p.96.

JONES, William and Ann Wortham, widow. Bond 22 February 1754. Sur. and Wit. William Bristow. p.8.

JONES, William and Betty Churchhill. Bond 23 November 1774. Sur. and Wit. John Smith. p.20.

JONES, William and Elizabeth Blade. Bond 17 January 1786. Sur. and Wit. Paulin Blackburn. p.29.

KEEBLE, Walter and Elizabeth Stapleton, spinster. Bond 29 November 1755. Sur. and Wit. Thomas Hardin and John Butterworth. p.9.

KEININGHAM (KENNINGHAM), Gideon and Margarett M. Johnson. Bond 1 January 1852. Married in January 1852 by Thomas B. Evans. Henry Johnson, father of Margarett. Sur. and Wit. Richard H. Johnson (or Henry Johnson) and John Milby. p. 116.

KELLMAN, Ezekiel and Catharine Garton. Bond 26 January 1834. Sur. and Wit. William Garton. p.113.

KELLUM, Able and Frances Jackson. Bond 28 November 1831. Married 1 December 1831 by George Northam. James Jackson gives consent. Sur. and Wit. John L. Jackson. p.106.

KELLUM, Abel and Mildred Kellum. Bond 27 October 1851. Married 28 October 1851 by R. H. Crittenden. Sur. and Wit. R. H. Crittenden and John A. Miles. p.141.

KELLUM, James H. and Harriett L. Hearn. Consent dated 21 September 1852 Abel Kellum, father of James. Elizabeth A. Hearn, mother of Harriett. Sur. and Wit. R. H. Crittenden. [Consent only.] p.142.

KELLUM, Richard H. and Elizabeth Greenwood. Married 4 January 1838 by George Northam. [Minister's return only.] p.161.

KEMP, Matthew and Lucy Daniel, upwards of 21 years. Bond 21 May 1801. Married 21 May 1801 by Henry Heffernan. Sur. and Wit. Thomas Muse, Jr. and Nancy Murray. p.52.

KEMP, Captain Peter and Hannah Kemp. Bond 5 February 1784. Mary Kemp, mother of Hannah. Sur. and Wit. Cary Kemp. p.27.

KEMP, Thomas and Miss Mary Spencer Smith. Bond 23 June 1755. Sur. and Wit. John Murray and James Webb, Jr. p.9.

KENNER, Rodham, Esq. and Elizabeth Plater, spinster. Bond 3 August 1763. George Plater, Esq., father of Elizabeth. Sur. and Wit. Ralph Wormeley, Esq. and Ralph Wormeley, Jr. p.15.

KENNINGHAM, William and Betty C. Trice. Bond 31 January 1843. Sur. and Wit. William H. Major and H. P. Montague. p.122.

KENT, Coleman and Miss Nancy Barrick. Bond 13 March 1827. William
Barrick, father of Nancy. Sur. and Wit. William Barrick. p.96.

KEY, James and Elizur A. (Elizar) Morris. Bond 6 December 1832.
Squire Morris, father of Elizur. Sur. and Wit. Thomas Key, Robert
Daniel, younger, and Frank Morris. p.109.

KEY, Thomas (free man of color) and Catharine Jackson. Bond 8 February. 1826. Sur. and Wit. James Key and Abraham Nekins. p.94.

KIDD, Alvin and Elizabeth Long. Bond 1 November 1827. Sur. and
Wit. William Baker. p.98.

KIDD, Burges and Sarah Daniel. Bond 22 July 1793. Sur. and Wit.
Nichols Tuggle. p.40.

KIDD, Chowning and Miss Catharine Thurston. Bond 21 December 1830.
Married 23 December 1830 by Richard Claybrook. Sur. and Wit.
Bachelder Owen. p.105.

KIDD, Churchhill and Miss Jane M. George. Bond 10 December 1824.
John George, deceased, father of Jane. Sur. and Wit. James Stamper.
p.90.

KIDD, Henry and Catharine Swords. Bond 23 October 1786. Sur. and Wit.
John Seward (or John Swords, Sr.) p.30.

KIDD, Isaac and Polly Kidd. Bond 17 December 1790. James Kidd, Sr.,
father of Polly. Sur. and Wit. Benjamin Kidd, Jr. p.36.

KIDD, Isaac and Miss Lucy Lee. Bond 19 August 1811. Reuben Lee,
deceased, father of Lucy; Thomas Trice, her guardian. Sur. and
Wit. Thomas Trice. p.72.

KIDD, James and Frances French. Bond 16 December 1795. Sur. and Wit.
Thomas Churchill and Staige Davis. p.44.

KIDD, James and Caty Mickelburrough. Bond 30 July 1795. Married
15 August 1795 by Henry Heffernan. Sur. and Wit. Isaac Kidd. p.43.

KIDD, James, 21 years of age, and Miss Sarah C. Bristow. Bond
9 December 1817. Catherine Kidd, mother of James. Bartholomew
Bristow, deceased, father of Sarah; George Healy, her guardian.
Sur. and Wit. Richard Garrett, Edward Bristow, and Meriker Kidd. p.83.

KIDD, James and Miss Harriet Sibley. Bond 11 August 1829. Holland
Walker, guardian of Harriet. Sur. and Wit. Chowning Kidd and Thomas
B. Evans. p.102.

KIDD, James and Frances Gardner. Bond 20 October 1847. Sur. and Wit.
Henry Sears and Leroy Seward. p.132.

KIDD, John and Elizabeth Wyatt. Bond 27 December 1813. Joseph Wyatt, deceased, father of Elizabeth. Sur. and Wit. Elijah Wyatt. p.76.

KIDD, Lody and Jane Kidd. Bond 22 December 1800. Benjamin Kidd, Sr., father of Jane. Sur. and Wit. Griffin Tuggle and John Kidd. p.52.

KIDD, Robert and Nancy Dillard. Bond 1 September 1800. George Kidd, father of Robert. George Dillard, father of Nancy. Sur. and Wit. John Brooks. p.51.

KIDD, Thomas and Ann Blakey, above 21 years of age. Bond 3 February 1801. Married 5 February 1801 by Henry Heffernan. Sur. and Wit. William C. Blakey. p.52.

KIDD, William and Rachel Chowning. Bond 1 August 1786. Sur. and Wit. Robert Chowning. p.30.

KIDD, William and Nancy Kidd. Bond 31 December 1788. Married 1 January 1789 by Samuel Klug. Sur. and Wit. Thomas Crittenden. p.34

KIDD, William and Sally Stamper. Bond 17 May 1793. Sur. and Wit. Leonard Stamper. p.40.

KIDD, William, Jr. and Lucy Williams, both of age. Bond 23 November 1802. Sur. and Wit. William Kidd, W. W. Cunningham, William Wake, and Thol. Wood. p.55.

KING, Thomas and Christiana Meggs. Bond 8 June 1816. Sur. and Wit. Robert Meggs and Edmund Jones. p.81.

LAMBRETH (LAMBETH), John and Catey Wyatt. Bond 16 December 1797. Richard Wyatt, father of Catey. Sur. and Wit. Thomas Trice and Churchill Blackburn. p.47.

LATHAM, Thomas and Caroline Smith. Bond 10 November 1758. Sur. and Wit. Maurice Smith. p.10.

LAUGHLIN, Simon and Ann Scrosby, widow. Bond 31 August 1772. Sur. and Wit. George Lorimer and Will. Churchhill. p.17.

LAYTON, Charles G. and Miss Elizabeth Wake, 21 years of age. Bond 17 January 1810. Sur. and Wit. Griffin Cundiff, John G. Wake, and Griffin F. Cundiff. p.69.

LAYTON, George and Catharine Adkinson, widow. Bond 19 May 1807. Married 20 May 1807 by Henry Heffernan. Sur. and Wit. Robert Barrick. p.64.

LAYTON, John, Sr., and Eliza Davis. Bond 10 March 1809. Sur. and Wit. A. New, Jr. p.67.

LAYTON, John, Jr., and Lucy Wilkins. Married 17 November 1796 by Henry Heffernan. [Minister's return only.] p.152.

LAYTON, Reuben and Martha Wilcox. Bond 14 February 1784. Sur. and Wit. John Adkerson. p.27.

LAYTON, Reuben and Elizabeth Burton. Bond 26 October 1786. Sur. and Wit. Charles Edwards. p.30.

LAYTON, Richard and Mrs. Elizabeth Woodley. Bond 26 February 1816. Elizabeth is the widow of John Woodley, deceased, and signs her own consent. Sur. and Wit. John Layton, Jr. p.80.

LAYTON, Thomas and Miss Mary Davis. Bond 5 May 1809. James Davis, deceased, father of Mary; Samuel B. Wood, her guardian. Sur. and Wit. Samuel B. Wood. p.67.

LAYTON, William and Mary Atkins. Bond 30 March 1797. Married 1 April 1797 by Henry Heffernan. Sur. and Wit. John Layton and Benjamin Bristow. p.46.

LEE, Charles and Joanna Morgan. Bond 7 May 1753. William Morgan, father of Joanna. Sur. and Wit. George Medlicott. p.7.

LEE, Charles, Jr. and Clarissa Montague. Bond 22 September 1806. Elizabeth Montague, mother of Clarissa, and also her guardian. Sur. and Wit. Elizabeth Montague. p.63.

LEE, Charles and Elizabeth Howard. Bond 15 April 1815. Allen Howard, deceased, father of Elizabeth. Sur. and Wit. William D. Shackelford. p.79.

LEE, Corrie and Miss Mildred Hutchings. Bond 25 December 1826. Sur. and Wit. Opie Hutchings and John C. New. p.96.

LEE, James and Elizabeth Daniel, widow. Bond 2 February 1774. Sur. and Wit. Zachariah Shackelford and Andrew McCan. p.19.

LEE, James and Frances Thurston. Bond 1 December 1789. Married 5 January 1790 by Samuel Klug. Robert Thurston, deceased, father of Frances. John Jackson gives consent. Sur. and Wit. Thomas Segar, Tobias Allen, and Allen Howard. p.35.

LEE, Killis and Miss Maria Parron. Bond 24 April 1817. William Parron, deceased, and Catherine Parron, parents of Maria. Sur. and Wit. Joseph McTyre. p.82.

LEE, Philip and Miss Nancy Jacobs. Bond 28 December 1815. Nancy signs own consent. Sur. and Wit. Benjamin Jacobs and Abraham Montague. p.80.

LEE, Reuben and Sarah Williams. Bond 7 May 1781. Sur. and Wit. Benjamin Kidd. p.25.

LEE, Richard and Elizabeth Vass. Bond 2 August 1792. Married 5 August 1792 by John Mullins. Sur. and Wit. Reuben Lee and Peter Robinson. p.39.

LEE, Richeson and Jane Abbot. Bond 25 October 1784. Sur. and Wit. Nichols Tuggle. p. 27.

LEE, Robert T. and Mrs. Elizabeth M. Healy, Bond 24 April 1817. Elizabeth is widow of James Healy, deceased, and signs her own consent. Sur. and Wit. Thomas Trice. p.83.

LEE, Robert T. and Miss Rebecca Trice, of lawful age. Bond 20 August 1824. Thomas Trice, father of Rebecca. Sur. and Wit. James Stamper. p.90.

LEE, William and Miss Elizabeth Hackney. Bond 28 January 1828. Married 28 January 1828 by Richard Claybrook. Catharine B. Hackney, mother of Elizabeth. Sur. and Wit. John Puller, John Owen, and Robert Trice. p.98.

LEE, William and Louisa E. Davis. Bond 7 January 1845. Sur. and Wit. James H. Hackney and William T. Hackney. p.127.

LEE, William H. and Mary E. Garrett. Bond 24 January 1848. Married 3 February 1848 by R. A. Christian. Sur. and Wit. William Lee and W. S. Hackney. p.133.

LETRELL, James M. and Eliza J. Pritchett. Bond 10 January 1850. Sur. and Wit. Samuel A. Pritchett and William L. Stakes(?). p.137.

LEWIS, John and Miss Lucy Hall. Bond 1 March 1832. Sur. and Wit. Henry Muse, Jr. and William Lewis. p.108.

LEWIS, John and Frances Ann Parker. Bond 19 February 1849. Married 20 February 1849 by Holland Walker. Sur. and Wit. Dudley Hosley and Sarah A. South. p.136.

LEWIS, Jonathan and Sarah Gale Morgan. Bond 9 August 1782. Sur. and Wit. Hugh Walker. p.26.

LEWIS. Thomas J. and Jane Spann. Bond 2 May 1829. Married between 2 July 1828 and 2 July 1829 by Nathan Healy. Sur. and Wit. William Lewis. p.101.

LEWIS, Thomas J. and Ann Miller. Married 13 July 1837 by George Northam. [Minister's return only.] p.161.

LEWIS, Thomas J. and Sarah F. Mason. Bond 12 April 1852. Married 15 April 1852 by Holland Walker. Sur. and Wit. James D. Crittenden and Mary A. Crittenden. p.142.

LEWIS, William and Miss Elizabeth Spann, orphan. Bond 27 March 1822. Sur. and Wit. Anthony Smith. p.86.

LIPSCOMB, Joseph M. and Miss Narcissa Elgar. Bond 10 June 1829. Sur. and Wit. George Healy and Phil^n Elgar. p.101.

LISLEY, Joseph, above 21 years, and Mrs. Nancy Blaid. Bond 21 November
1808. Nancy is widow of Isaac Blake. Sur. and Wit. John Mason and
James Cundiff. p.67.

LOKMON, Richard of Essex County, and Betty Bryant, widow. Bond 3 November 1761. Sur. and Wit. John Yarrington and Robert Elliot. p.13.

LONG, David and Miss Susanna Green, 21 years of age. Bond 30 March
1830. Married 25 March 1830 by George Northam. Thomas J. Green
signs affidavit as to Susanna's age. Sur. and Wit. Samuel B. Wood.
p.103.

LONG, John and Miss Louisa M. Daniel. Bond 25 January 1830. Married
3 February 1830 by George Northam. Sur. and Wit. George Healy. p.102.

LONG, John Blake and Sarah Blake. Bond 29 December 1798. Married
30 December 1798 by Henry Heffernan. Sur. and Wit. Warner Blake and
Hannah Harrison Jones. p.49.

LONG, John B. and Martha Major. Bond 31 October 1814. Sur. and Wit.
Warner C. Blake. p.78.

LONG, Robert and Johanna Blake. Bond 20 June 1798. Married 5 July 1798
by Henry Heffernan. Sur. and Wit. Augustine Blake. p.48.

LONG, Robert, Jr. and Miss Eliza Robinson. Bond 17 July 1833. Married
22 July 1833 by George Northam. Sur. and Wit. Robert Long, Sr. p.111.

LONGEST, William and Mary Davis. Married 29 January 1795 by John Healy.
[Minister's return only.] p.146.

LORIMER, George and Hannah Thacker Timberlake. Bond 3 October 1774.
Mary Elizabeth Thacker, aunt and guardian, appointed by New Kent
County Court. Sur. and Wit. James Mills, Mary Yates, and James Kidd.
p.20.

LOW, Andrew and Mary Roane. Bond 3 July 1765. Sur. and Wit. Charles
Roane and John Yarrington. p.16.

LYN, Henry and Ann Parrot. Bond 27 July 1782. Sur. and Wit. Simon
Laughlin. p.26.

MACHAN, James and Mary Madieras. Bond 5 January 1762. Sur. and Wit.
James Daniel. p.13.

MACKAN, Horace M. and Penelope D. Cloudis. Bond 15 January 1846. Sur.
and Wit. William W. Stone and Ellison Daniel. p.130.

MAJOR, John and Mary Murray, who is upward of twenty-one years of age.
Bond 3 February 1802. Married 6 February 1802 by Henry Heffernan.
Sur. and Wit. Thomas Spann and Dawson Hudgins. p.54.

MAJOR, John A. and Miss Julia Ann Humphries. Bond 9 February 1825.
Nelson Humphries, deceased, father of Julia. John B. Garland signs
affidavit that Julia was of age March 1824. Sur. and Wit. Benjamin
E. Bristow. p.91.

MAJOR, Matthew and Miss Elizabeth Blakey. Bond 30 January 1808.
Churchill Blakey, father of Elizabeth. Married 30 January 1808 by
Henry Heffernan. Sur. and Wit. Thomas Kidd, Frances Blakey, and
Lucy Blakey. p.66.

MAJOR, Robert S. and Miss Lucy B. Bristow. Bond 26 January 1832. Lucy
is orphan of Leonard Bristow. Sur. and Wit. Lewis S. Bristow and
Warner Roane. p.107.

MALLORY, Edward and Miss Lucy Ann Chapman. Bond 14 October 1833.
Married 14 October 1833 by George Northam. Sur. and Wit. William
C. Chapman. p.112.

MARCHANT, Thomas and Lucy Dudley. Bond 16 February 1797. Sur. and
Wit. John Sutton. p.46.

MASON, John and Sarah N. Wood. Bond 18 January 1806. Married 18 January 1806 by William Frichett of Mathews County. Elizabeth Wood
gives consent. Sur. and Wit. Robert Barrick and George W. Layton.
p.61.

MASON, Lemuel and Martha Ann Berry. Bond 11 March 1850. Married
12 March 1850 by Holland Walker. Sur. and Wit. George W. Daniel and
Thomas N. Bull. p. 130.

MASON, Lemuel and Susan J. Berry. Bond 5 July 1851. Married 4 July
1851 by Holland Walker. Sur. and Wit. Norborn Mason and William
Shreeves. p.140.

MASON, Miles F. and Frances Garrett. Bond 8 December 1837. Sur. and
Wit. Mickelborough Daniel. p.117.

MASON, Miles F. and Anna D. Dickie. Married December 1852 by Thomas B.
Evans. [Minister's return only.] p.166.

MASON, Norman and Miss Maria Ailsworth. Bond 13 April 1844. Married
24 April 1844 by George Norman. Sur. and Wit. Josiah D. Ailsworth
and Lenox Ailsworth. p.125.

MATTHEWS, Henry L. and Ann E. Palmer. Bond 17 December 1849. Married
20 December 1849 by Holland Walker, with personal consent of Ann's
father. Sur. and Wit. Lewis Palmer. p.137.

MATTHEWS, Moses and Lucy Wake. Bond 27 April 1799. Lucy is widow of
Johnson Wake. Sur. and Wit. Stanton B.Dudley and Peter Kemp,Jr. p.49.

MATTHEWS, Moses and Hannah Humphries, above 21 years. Bond 20 October
1808. Sur. and Wit. William Matthews and John Jackson. p.67.

MATHEWS, Moses and Lucy Harrow. Married 19 July 1838 by George Northam.
[Minister's return only.] p.161.

MATTHEWS, William and Elen Hunt. Bond 7 October 1791. Sur. and Wit.
William Wood, Jr. p.37.

MATTHEWS, William and Mary Burton. Bond 6 February 1804. Married
6 February 1804 by William Frichett of Mathews County. Sur. and
Wit. Thomas Burke and William Norton. p.57.

MATTHEWS, William and Miss Rachel Sharod. Married 9 July 1841 by Lewis
H. Williams. [Minister's return only.] p.164.

McCUDDIN, George and Miss Mary Elizabeth Oaks. Bond 11 November 1845.
Sarah R. Oaks, mother of Mary. Sur. and Wit. George Bright and Henry
Dickerson. p.129.

McDONALD, James and Adeline F. Blakey. Bond 28 June 1848. Sur. and
Wit. Richard F. Rowzee, John C. Blakey, and Adeline Blakey. p. 134.

McGILL, John D. and Miss Matilda Ann Elizabeth Temple Woodward. Bond
29 August 1827. Married 6 September 1827 by Richard Claybrook.
Richard Woodward, father of Matilda. Sur. and Wit. Francis Smith. p.97.

McINTIRE, George M. and Miss Louisa A. Davis. Bond 28 February 1816.
Staige Davis, deceased, father of Louisa. Sur. and Wit. Walter
Healy. p.81.

McKAN, Henry and Miss Eleanor C. Daniel. Bond 18 September 1829.
Sur. and Wit. Robert Daniel, Sr. p.102.

McKAN, John and Jenny Daniel. Bond 22 October 1787. Married 2 November 1787 by John Mullins. Sur. and Wit. Charles Lee, Jr. p.31.

McKAN, Philip and Molly Owen, of lawful age. Bond 11 November 1802.
Sur. and Wit. Leonard Jackson. p.55.

McTYRE, George and Miss Priscilla Taff. Bond 22 December 1829. Sur.
and Wit. Joseph McTyre and Richard H. Street, who swears Priscilla
is above 21 years. p. 102.

McTYRE, Josiah (or Joseph) and Nancy Daniel. Bond 4 July 1800. Henry
McTyre, father of Josiah. Elizabeth Daniel, mother of Nancy. Sur.
and Wit. Lewis Montague. p.51.

McTYRE, Joseph and Mary Haile. Bond 24 April 1824. Sur. and Wit.
John C. Montague and Ann Montague. p.89.

McTYRE, Larkin C. and Elizabeth George, of age. Bond 17 February 1824.
William George, deceased, father of Elizabeth. Joseph McTyre gives
consent for Larkin. Sur. and Wit. Mickelborough Daniel and William
Wortham. p.89.

McTYRE, William D. and Miss Catharine M. Parron. Bond 23 June 1826.
William Parron, father of Catharine. Sur. and Wit. Joseph McTyree,
Caty Dawson. p.95.

MEACHAM, Lawrence and Frances Batcheldor. Bond 1 February 1773. Sur.
and Wit. Simon Laughlin and John McNikal. p.17.

MEACHAM, William and Jane Aldin, widow. Bond 25 January 1748. Sur.
and Wit. Edward Dillard, Thomas Price, and Richard Major. p.4.

MEACHAM, Wortham and Mary Bristow, of age. Bond 5 January 1802. Sur.
and Wit. Leonard Bristow. p.54.

MEACHAN (MACHAN), James and Casandra Warwick, widow. Bond 25 February
1744. Sur. and Wit. Humphrey Jones and Lewis Mountague. p.2.

MEARS, John W. and Amanda Walden. Bond 23 December 1850. Married
31 December 1850 by R. A. Christian. Sur. and Wit. Joseph Walden
and Joseph H. Walden. p.139.

MEGGES (MEGGS), James and Mary Wilson. Bond 29 December 1780. Ruth
Wilson, mother of Mary. Sur. and Wit. William Dawson, William
Naughtin and Francis King. p.24.

MERCER, John L. and Louisa Walden. Bond 14 June 1852. Married 22 June
1852 by Holland Walker. Thomas Trice, guardian, consents. Sur. and
Wit. James C. Mercer and Joseph H. Walden. p.142.

MICKELBOROUGH, Edmond H. and Mary E. Parron. Bond 14 February 1848.
Holland M. Parron, guardian of Mary. Sur. and Wit. W. L. Mickelborough
and Zach Street. p.133.

MICKELBOROUGH, James and Charlotte Ann Trice. Bond 22 July 1839. Sur.
and Wit. William Garrett and Philip Montague, Jr. p.119.

MICKELBOROUGH, Lewis L., under age, and Miss Henrietta Haile. Bond
30 October 1823. Lewis Mickelborough, father of Lewis. Wheeler
Haile, deceased, father of Henrietta. Sur. and Wit. John Haile,
Thomas Haile, and Abraham Montague. p.88.

MICKELBURROUGH, Henry and Susanna Street. Bond 23 November 1795.
Susanna is orphan of Richard Street, deceased. John Saddler of
Essex County, guardian, and gives consent. Sur. and Wit. William
Montague and Lewis Montague. p.44.

MICKELBURROUGH, James and Susanna Daniel. Bond 22 May 1797. Sary
Cloudas, mother of Susanna. Sur. and Wit. Travis Daniel and
William Jones. p.46.

MICKELBURROUGH, John and Caty Allen. Bond 15 March 1785. Sur. and
Wit. Tobias Allen. p.28.

MICKELBURROUGH, Lewis and Elizabeth Lee. Bond 27 July 1795. Married 15 August 1795 by Robert Ware. Philip Lee, father of Elizabeth, gives consent. Sur. and Wit. Travis Daniel. p.43.

MICKELBOROUGH, Richard and Laura A. F. Trice. Bond 27 May 1850. Sur. and Wit. Robert T. Thrift. p.138.

MICKELBURROUGH, Robert and Elizabeth Dean. Bond 22 November 1791. Sur. and Wit. John Dean. p.37.

MILBEY, Richard H. and Miss Maria D. Bristow. Bond 4 January 1823. Josiah Bristow, father of Maria. Sur. and Wit. Henry Milbey and Elizabeth D. Bristow. p.86.

MILBEY, William and Mary S. Seward. Bond 17 February 1835. George Saunders, guardian of Mary. Sur. and Wit. John C. Montague. p.115.

MILBY, James and Frances Ross. Bond 10 April 1790. Married 11 April 1790 by Samuel Klug. Sur. and Wit. Francis Ross. p.35.

MILBY, Robert and Dorothea M. Trice. Bond 22 December 1851. Married in December 1851 by Thomas B. Evans. Sur. and Wit. George Saunders. p.141.

MILBY, William and Miss Elizabeth Thurston. Bond 27 December 1824. Sur. and Wit. Henry Thurston. p.91

MILBY, William and Jane Hall. Bond 20 December 1839. Sur. and Wit. Robert Haile. p.119.

MILES, John A. and Miss Judith Jackson. Bond 21 December 1807. Married 21 December 1807 by David Corey. Sur. and Wit. James Jackson. p.65.

MILES, John A. and Mary V. Hillyard. Bond 25 November 1844. B. R. Hillyard, father of Mary. Sur. and Wit. James H. Jackson and John R. Creighton. p. 126.

MILES, William F. and Lauretta Creighton. Married in April 1846 by John J. Boss. [Minister's return only.] p.168.

MILES, William T. and Miss Loretta Creighton. Bond 6 April 1846. Robert Healy, guardian of William, writes his consent from New Market. John R. Creighton, father of Loretta, writes his consent from Woodstock. Sur. and Wit. John R. Pace, James H. Jackson, and John A. Miles. p.130. [Apparently same as above.]

MILLER, Christopher A. and Miss Elenor Walker. Bond 13 January 1845. Married 16 January 1845 by George Northam. Sur. and Wit. William J. Bennett. p.127.

MILLER, Dabney and Catharine Dunn. Bond 10 May 1802. Agrippa Dunn, father of Catharine. Sur. and Wit. Agrippa Dunn. p.54.

MILLER, Dabney A. and Miss Mary Saunders, above 21 years. Bond 7 March 1808. Sur. and Wit. John Saunders. p.66.

MILLER, Isham and Miss Nancy Dunlavey. Bond 23 March 1812. Braxton Dunlavey, father of Nancy. Sur. and Wit. Braxton Dunlavey. p.74.

MILLER, James and Miss Nancy Ware. Bond 24 November 1827. Reubin Ware, father of Nancy. Sur. and Wit. James Chowning and Richard C. Muse. p.98.

MILLER, John and Hester Christian. Bond 8 December 1774. Sur. and Wit. Hugh Walker. p.20.

MILLER, John and Avarilla Saunders. Bond 22 October 1792. Sur. and Wit. Peter Robinson. p.39.

MILLER, John and Miss Eliza Wake. Bond 13 November 1817. Sur. and Wit. Isham Miller. p.83.

MILLER, John D. and Mary Elizabeth Mercer. Bond 8 May 1849. Married 9 May 1849 by Holland Walker, with personal consent of father of Mary [his name not given.] Sur. and Wit. James Mercer. p.136.

MINTER, Bowler and Mary Matthews. Bond 16 June 1792. Sur. and Wit. Stanton Dudley and Peter Robinson. p.38.

MINTER, John P. and Sarah Jones. Bond 15 September 1847. Married 16 September 1847 by George Northam. Sur. and Wit. Robert L. Montague. p.132.

MINTER, Thomas and Martha Turner. Bond 29 August 1797. Martha Turner, Sr., mother of Martha. Sur. and Wit. John Clarke, Jr. and Hudson Muse. p.47.

MITCHELL, John and Sarah Batcheldor. Bond 28 February 1774. John George gives consent for Sarah. Sur. and Wit. Laurence Meacham, Jasper Clayton, and James Kidd. p.20.

MONTAGUE, Aeneas and Miss Maria Ann Catharine Blakey. Bond 20 September 1831. Sur. and Wit. Robert Blakey. p.106.

MONTAGUE, Abraham R. and Jane Lee, single and of age. Bond 22 September 1806. Ann Lee, mother of Jane. Sur. and Wit. Philip T. Montague and William L. Montague. p.63.

MONTAGUE, Augustas F. and Miss Frances Ware. Bond 14 February 1831. Sur. and Wit. Thomas Hundley, Jr. p.105.

MONTAGUE, Augustus F. and Mrs. Lucy H. Kemp. Bond 15 July 1840. Lucy is widow of Levi H. Kemp. Sur. and Wit. Leonard Perry. p.120.

MONTAGUE, Edmond H. and Miss Amanda (C.) Claybrook(e). Bond 1 November 1832. Richard Claybrook, father of Amanda. Sur. and Wit. Thomas Muse. p. 109.

MONTAGUE, Henry P. and Mary M. Trice. Married 1 April 1841 by Richard A. Christian. p.164.

MONTAGUE, John Curry and Charlotte Montague. Bond 25 February 1788. Married 25 March 1788 by Samuel Klug. Sur. and Wit. Thomas Montague. p.32.

MONTAGUE, John C. and Mrs. Frances Howard. Bond 16 December 1830. Sur. and Wit. Thomas Jesse. p.105.

MONTAGUE, John C. and Miss Ann Lee. Bond 22 December 1812. Charles Lee, guardian of Ann. Sur. and Wit. Thomas G. Crittenden, Robert C. Ware, and Abraham Montague. p.76.

MONTAGUE, John L. and Miss Sarah Jane McTyre. Bond 30 December 1846. Mary McTyre, mother of Sarah. Sur. and Wit. Robert L. Montague, James R. Montague, and Joseph Haile. p.131.

MONTAGUE, Latane and Catherine Montague, of lawful age. Bond 9 April 1811. Married 9 April 1811 by Philip Montague. Sur. and Wit. Abraham Montague and Richard Claybrook. p. 72.

MONTAGUE, Lewis B. and Miss Catherine Jesse. Bond 2 June 1817. John Jesse, deceased, father of Catherine. Sur. and Wit. Richard Claybrook. p.84.

MONTAGUE, Philip, of Essex County, and Martha Montague. Bond 6 April 1803. Philip Montague, Sr., guardian of Martha. Sur. and Wit. William L. Montague. p.56.

MONTAGUE, Philip and Frances Lee. Bond 28 May 1810. Philip Lee, deceased, father of Frances. Sur. and Wit. Charles Lee. p.70.

MONTAGUE, Robert H. and Frances A. Jones. Bond 23 June 1851. Sur. and Wit. William R. Jones. p.140.

MONTAGUE, Samuel and Elizabeth S. Montague, of age 21. Bond 9 July 1799. Married 11 July 1799 by Henry Heffernan. Sur. and Wit. William Montague. p.50.

MONTAGUE, Thomas and Catharine Vass. Married 22 December 1787 by Samuel Klug. [Minister's return only.] p. 147.

MONTAGUE, Thomas and Ann Healy. Bond 27 January 1795. Thomas Healy, father of Ann, gives consent. Sur. and Wit. William B. Lewis. p.42.

MONTAGUE, Thomas A. and Lucy Dunn. Bond 25 December 1848. James
Dunn gives consent for Lucy. Sur. and Wit. William H. Daniel and
John P. Dunn. p.136.

MONTAGUE, Thomas T. and Elizabeth Montague. Bond 27 October 1801.
Married 19 December 1801 by Henry Heffernan. Sur. and Wit. Samuel
Montague. p.53.

MONTAGUE, William and Elizabeth Valentine. Bond 1 December 1789.
Married 14 January 1790 by Samuel Klug. Sur. and Wit. James Lee.
p.35.

MONTAGUE, William and Frances Street. Bond 23 September 1793. Sur.
and Wit. John Street and George Dame. p.40.

MONTAGUE, William, of lawful age, and Penelope Lee, of lawful age.
Bond 26 October 1802. Francis Montague, father of William.
Philip Lee, father of Penelope. Sur. and Wit. Philip Montague,
Charles Lee, and Philip Montague, Jr. p.55.

MONTAGUE, William V. and Miss Mary Ann Barrick. Bond 15 December 1824.
Robert Barrick, Esq., father of Mary Ann. Sur. and Wit. Robert
Barrick. p.90.

MONTGOMERY, James and Miss Elizabeth Read. Bond 2 October 1833. Sur.
and Wit. Morris Montgomery. p.112.

MONTGOMERY, Morris and Mrs. Nancy Read, widow. Bond 23 October 1832.
Sur. and Wit. Henry Wroten [Martin on bond.] p.109.

MONTGOMERY, Seth and Hester Ann Christopher [Nancy on bond.] Bond
24 November 1845. Married 24 November 1845 by John J. Boss. Nancy
Christopher, mother of Hester. Sur. and Wit. James Dudley and
Moris Montgomery. p.129.

MONTGOMERY, Stith and Sarah Davis. Bond 10 May 1852. Sur. and Wit.
Robert J. Boss and John J. Boss. p.142.

MOODY, Burgess S. and Harriott Corey. Bond 28 October 1805. Married
28 October 1805 by William Frichett of Mathews County. David Corey,
father of Harriott. Sur. and Wit. David Corey. p.60.

MOORE, George and Miss Catherine Bennett, of lawful age. Bond 5 November 1820. Sur. and Wit. John B. Garland. p.85.

MOORE, George and Mrs. Mary Brown. Bond 2 July 1828. Married between
2 July 1828 and 2 July 1829 by Nathan Healy. Sur. and Wit. Enos
Healy. p.99.

MOORE, William and Elizabeth Swords. Bond 28 February 1780. Sur. and
Wit. Peter Montague. p.23.

MORE, Samuel and Martha Davis. Bond 22 March 1781. Sur. and Wit.
Matthias Fox. p.24

MORGAN, John and Mary Katharine Mountague. Bond 29 July 1761. William
Mountague, deceased, father of Mary. Sur. and Wit. Benjamin Rhodes,
Robert Elliot, and Dorothy Rhodes. p.12.

MORGAN, John and Lucy Hardin, widow. Bond 22 March 1765. Sur. and
Wit. Rowland Sutton and Eliza. Elliot. p.16.

MORRIS, Frank and Martha Kee. Bond 25 January 1844. P. T. Montague
gives affidavit that Martha is of lawful age. Martha has three
children. Sur. and Wit. Squire Morris. p.125.

MORRIS, Squire and Elizabeth Key. Bond 18 December 1832. Sur. and
Wit. Thomas Key, James Key and Philip Montague, Jr. p.110.

MOSS, George and Martha Boss. Consent dated 12 October 1745. Eliza
Boss, mother of Martha. Sur. and Wit. A. H. Crittenden. p. 143.

MOULSON, William and Mary Segar. Bond 26 July 1745. Oliver Segar, deceased, father of Mary; Jane Dudley, mother. Sur. and Wit. Chr.
Curtis, Jane Segar, and Judith Segar. p.3.

MOUNTAGUE, John and Catherine Yates. Bond 25 November 1776. Sur. and
Wit. Samuel Mountague and Jasper Clayton. p.21.

MOUNTAGUE, Philip, bachelor and Frances Mountague, spinster. Bond 3 May
1763. Sur. and Wit. Lewis Mountague. p.14.

MOUNTAGUE, Richard and Charlotte Mountague. Bond 27 February 1786.
Sur. and Wit. Thomas Mountague. p.29.

MOUNTAGUE, Thomas and Ann Batchelder. Bond 20 March 1780 [shown in
register as 1783.] Sur. and Wit. Henry Vass. p. 27

MOUNTAGUE, Thomas and Catharine Vass. Bond 20 December 1787. Sur. and
Wit. Richard Mountague. p.32.

MOUNTAGUE, William and Catharine Mountague. Bond 21 December 1754.
Sur. and Wit. Lewis Mountague. p.8.

MOUNTAIN, John B. and Elizabeth Jones. Bond 20 December 1800. Married
26 December 1800 by Henry Heffernan. Sur. and Wit. John Barrock. p.51.

MOUNTAIN, Robert T. and Mrs. Rosa Jones [Rosy Clare on consent.]
Bond 4 February 1833. Married 5 February 1833 by George Northam,
who gives the name Rosa Clare. Sur. and Wit. Major Bird and B.
Clare. p.111.

60

MOUNTAIN, Robert T. and Susan S. Noel. Bond 3 March 1852. Married 3 March 1852 by Holland Walker. Sur. and Wit. Richerson Slaughter and Walter Major. p.141.

MULLINS, John and Ruth Greenwood. Bond 23 July 1787. Married 31 July 1787 by James Greenwood. Sur. and Wit. Edward Ware. p.31.

MULLINS, Thomas and Lucy Jesse. Bond 25 April 1806. William Jesse, deceased, father, John Jesse, guardian of Lucy. Sur. and Wit. Thomas Wilson and Jos. McTyre. p.62.

MURE (MUSE), George and Mrs. Priscilla Dudley. Bond 30 June 1832. Priscilla is widow of George Dudley, deceased. Sur. and Wit. John R. Potter and Moris Montgomery. p.109.

MURE, Henry and Matilda Davis. Bond 1 April 1834. Sur. and Wit. William Christopher. p.114.

MURRAY, Alexander, bachelor, and Mary Clark, spinster. Bond 14 October 1752. Sur. and Wit. John Murray and W. Young. p.7.

MURRAY, John and Jane Segar. Bond October 29, 1747. Sur. and Wit. William Moulson and Richard Major. p.4.

MURRAY, John and Miss Rachel Daniel. Bond 3 January 1750. Sur. and Wit. Samuel Wood. p.5.

MURRAY, John and Lucy Sutton. Bond 24 December 1798. Married 25 December 1798 by Henry Heffernan. Sur. and Wit. John Sutton. p.49.

MURRAY, Robert and Mary Skelton, spinster. Bond 21 December 1754. Sur. and Wit. John Taylor and William Eastham. p.8.

MURRAY, William and Ann Kemp. Bond 15 December 1779. Sur. and Wit. George Daniel. p.23.

MUSE, Elliott and Betty Tayloe Corbin, widow. Bond 3 May 1800. Married 3 May 1800 by Henry Heffernan. Sur. and Wit. John Chew. p.51.

MUSE, Hudson, Esq. and Miss Agnes Nielson. Bond 28 December 1790. Charlotte Nielsen, mother of Agnes. Sur. and Wit. James Spark. p.36.

MUSE, John James and Eglantine E. Cauthorne. Bond 8 March 1849. Married __ March 1849 by Thomas B. Evans. Sur. and Wit. Pearson Cauthorne and William Keiningham. p. 136.

MUSE, Lawrence and Jane Southall. Bond 30 May 1793. Sur. and Wit. John Muse and P. Kemp. p.40.

MUSE, Neilson and Miss Louisa M. Major. Bond 9 June 1826. Married 10 June 1826 by Richard Claybrook. John A. Major, father of Louisa. Sur. and Wit. James Stamper, Harriet J. Major, and Philander Elgar. p.95.

MUSE, Richard J. and Miss Anna Maria Wake. Bond 2 May 1831. Married
20 May 1831 by George Northam. Ambrose Wake, deceased, father,
and George S. Pace, guardian, of Anna. Sur. and Wit. Chancery G.
Griswold and Aeoneas Montague. p.105.

MUSE, Thomas and Harriot Murray, spinster. Bond 9 September 1799.
Married 16 September 1799 by Henry Heffernan. Charles Curtis
consents for Thomas. Sur. and Wit. Peter Kemp, Jr. p.50.

NELSON, Philip and Sarah Nelson Burwell. Married 27 January 1789.
by Samuel Klug. [Minister's return only.] p.149.

NEW, James and Lucy Barrick. Bond 27 December 1847. Married 28 December 1847 by R. A. Christian. Sur. and Wit. John C. New and
Thomas S. Brown. p.133.

NEW, John C. and Miss Mary Ann S. Barrick. Bond 25 December 1826.
Sur. and Wit. J. Stamper and Bailey Barrick. p.96.

NEWCOMB, William, Jr. and Elizabeth Roane. Bond 28 August 1797.
Married 4 September 1797 by LeRoy Cole. Sur. and Wit. William
Newcomb and William Kiningham. p.47.

NICOLNSON, George L. and Miss Frances L. Wyatt. Bond 6 October 1840.
James Wyatt, deceased, father of Frances. Sur. and Wit. Patrick H.
Fitzhugh and Thomas W. Fauntleroy. p.121.

NIELSON, Charles and Charlotte Washington, widow. Bond 26 October 1765.
Sur. and Wit. Ja. Gregorie, Francis Foushee, and Robert Spratt. p.16.

NOEL, Gilson and Jane Shipley. Bond 21 December 1797. Nathan Shipley,
father of Jane. Sur. and Wit. Samuel Shipley and Churchill Blackburn. p.47.

NOEL, James L. and Susannah S. Humphreys. Bond 11 June 1849. Margaret
S. Humphreys, mother of Susannah. Sur. and Wit. Richard S.
Mickelborough. p.136.

NORRIS, James and Virginia Jackson. Married 28 December 1842 by George
Northam. [Minister's return only.] p.162.

NORTHAM, Henry C. and Susan H. Hackney. Bond 24 November 1851. Married
24 November 1851 by R. A. Christian. "Issued by consent of father,"
but name not shown. Sur. and Wit. William S. Hackney. p.141.

NORTHAM, Zorababel and Cordelia Walker. Bond 15 May 1827. Sur. and
Wit. Holland Walker and Moses Walker, Sen. p.97.

NORTHAM, Zorobabel and Sarah E. Dunlavy. Certificate dated 10 July
1852. Married 22 July 1852 by Holland Walker. Sur. and Wit. John
W. Mears. p. 142.

NORTHAM, Zorobabel and Elizabeth Norton. Bond 15 June 1847. Married
__ June 1847 by George Northam. Sur. and Wit. George H. Northam
and John Mason. p.132.

NORTON, John and Mary Ann Cundiff. Married 15 November 1837 by George
Northam. [Minister's return only.] p.161.

NORTON, John and Miss Sarah Hall, above 21 years. Bond 20 October
1845. Married 20 October 1845 by Richard A. Christian. Sur. and
Wit. R. A. Christian, Jr. and Joseph Christian. p. 129.

NORTON, William, widower, and Miss Nancy Hill. Bond 18 January 1810.
William Hill, father of Nancy. Sur. and Wit. William Hill. p.69.

NORTON, William and Miss Elizabeth Mason. Bond 14 October 1833. Sur.
and Wit. John Mason. p.112.

NORTON, William H. and Jane Montgomery. Bond 15 June 1838. Married
13 June 1838 by George Northam. Sur. and Wit. James Pritchett. p.117.

NORTON, William L. and Miss Harriet Hart. Bond 8 November 1830. Married 17 November 1830 by George Northam. Richard Hart, father of
Harriet. Sur. and Wit. Henry Wroten. p.104.

OAKES, Major and Sally R. Daniel, 21 years old. Bond 28 March 1814.
Chesley Daniel, deceased, father of Sally. Sur. and Wit. William
Oakes, Linsey Clark, and Major Turner. p.77.

O'HARROW, Anthony and Fanny Vaughan. Bond 3 July 1802. Dudley Vaughan,
father of Fanny. Sur. and Wit. William Hill and Molly Garton. p.54.

O'HARROW, Martin and Elizabeth Vaughan. Bond 26 January 1807. Sur.
and Wit. David Corey. p.63.

OLIVER, Francis and Frances Cloudas. Bond 3 November 1800. Sur. and
Wit. Beverley Cloudas. p.51.

OLIVER, Francis and Nancy Ware. Bond 28 March 1804. Sur. and Wit.
Beverley Cloudas, Jack Montague, and Frances Cloudas. p.58.

OLIVER, Jesse and Mary Forest. Bond 26 May 1851. Sur. and Wit. Thomas
R. Bull. p.140.

OLIVER, Wilson and Elizabeth Lee, above 21 years. Bond 7 October 1806.
Sur. and Wit. Christopher Owen, Major Wyatt, and Gravely Oliver. p.63.

O'NEAL, Thomas, of King William County and Miss Mary Garland. Bond
14 January 1829. Sur. and Wit. Robert King. p. 100.

OSBORNE, Michael and Ann Bower. Bond 3 January 1778. Sur. and Wit.
Richard Bray. p.21.

OWEN, Augustine and Miss Almira Seward, of lawful age. Bond 25 November 1825. Married 25 November 1825 by Richard Claybrook. Sur. and Wit. Richard A. Christian. p.93.

OWEN, James and Winney Bennett. Bond 22 January 1798. Married 27 January 1798 by Henry Heffernan. Sur. and Wit. Thomas Bray and Henry Garrett. p.48.

OWEN, John and Polly Wyatt. Bond 20 September 1806. Joseph Wyatt, father of Polly. Sur. and Wit. Joseph Wyatt and Major Wyatt. p.62.

OWEN, John and Miss Catherine Montague. Bond 23 December 1811. Married 24 December 1811 by Philip Montague. William Montague, deceased, father and Chur[1]. Blakey, guardian, of Catherine. Sur. and Wit. Charles Lee. p.73.

OWEN, John and Miss Catherine Roane. Bond 5 September 1821. Thomas Roane, deceased, father of Catherine. Sur. and Wit. Robert Healy, Mira Ann Muse. p.85.

OWEN, John, Jr. and Miss Sarah E. R. Blakey. Bond 14 May 1830. Sur. and Wit. Robert Blakey. p.104.

OWEN, Robert C. and Miss Lucy Richardson. Bond 8 March 1830. Sur. and Wit. Thomas Street and Lucia S. Stiff. p.103.

OWEN, William and Miss Mary Fearn. Bond 9 February 1742. John Fearn, father of Mary. Sur. and Wit. John Fearn, Tho. Price, and Luke Burford. p. 1.

OWEN, William and Miss Lucy Williamson. Bond 22 February 1830. Sur. and Wit. Richard H. Street and Edwin Greenwood. p.103.

OWEN, William and Elizabeth Meacham. Bond 30 December 1748. Sur. and Wit. John Meacham and John Prentis. p.4.

OWEN, William and Jane Batcheldor. Bond 30 December 1777. Sur. and Wit. John Humphries. p.21.

OWEN, William and Bethuel Beddoo. Bond 29 October 1833. Laurence Beddoo, deceased, father of Bethuel. Sur. and Wit. John Owen. p.112.

PACE, Benjamin R. and Sarah Baker, "more than 21 years". Bond 2 February 1811. James Baker, Sr., deceased, father of Sarah. Sur. and Wit. Thomas Bray. p.72.

PACE, George D. and Miss Louisa Barrick. Bond 11 December 1832. Robert Barrick, father of Louisa. Sur. and Wit. Robert C. Garland. p.110.

PACE, George S. and Mrs. Mary Wake. Bond 14 June 1808. Married 15 February 1808 by David Corey. Sur. and Wit. David Corey and Jeris. Powell. p.66.

PACE, John R. and Amanda Pool. Bond 15 January 1850. Married 23 January 1850 by Holland Walker. Sur. and Wit. Robert H. Walker. p.138.

PACE, William and Crissy Sanders. Bond 29 October 1773. Benjamin Pace, father of William. Sur. and Wit. George Sanders and William Jones. p.18.

PAGE, Mann, Esq., of Rosewell, Gloucester County, and Miss Alice Grymes. Bond 29 December 1741. The Hon. John Grymes, Esq., father of Alice. Sur. and Wit. Robert Burwell. p. 1.

PAGE, Robert and Miss Sarah Walker. Bond 18 January 1749. John Walker, Gent., deceased, father of Sarah. Ch^r. Robinson, William Taliaferro, Alexander Frazier, give consent. Sur. and Wit. Bartholomew Yates, Chr. Curtis, P. Robinson, Jno. Taliaferro, Charles Moulson, James Reid, and Adam Reid. p.5.

PALMER, Alfred and Matilda B. Chowning. Married __ July 1841 by Richard A. Christian. [Minister's return only.] p.164.

PALMER, John D., single, born in Middlesex, and Mary F. Davis, single. Married 15 December 1853 by Holland Walker at Richard A. Davis'. Thomas J. and Polly Palmer, parents of John. Richard A. and Elizabeth B. Davis, parents of Mary. [Minister's return only.] p.170.

PALMER, John W. and Elizabeth C. Major. Bond 10 December 1838. Elizabeth Major, mother and guardian of Elizabeth. Sur. and Wit. Augustine Owen, Thomas Trice, and Ann Williams. p.117.

PALMER, Lewis and Miss Elizabeth J. Barrick. Bond 26 June 1832. William Barrick, father of Elizabeth. Sur. and Wit. William Barrick. p.108.

PALMER, Lewis and Miss Martha J. Green. Bond 2 January 1847. Married 3 January 1847 by R. A. Christian. Sur. and Wit. Thomas J. Bland. p.131.

PALMER, Thomas J. and Miss Polly A. Miller. Bond 20 November 1812. Sur. and Wit. John Miller. p.75.

PALMER, Thomas J. and Mary A. E. Palmer. Bond 23 December 1850. Married 24 December 1850 by R. A. Christian. H. C. Palmer, parent of Mary. Sur. and Wit. Alfred Palmer. p.140.

PALMER, Opie and Nancy F. Wortham, 21 years of age. Bond 19 December 1814. John Wortham, deceased, father, Catherine Wortham, mother, of Nancy. Sur. and Wit. Thomas J. Palmer and Henry Muse, Jr. p.78.

PARKER, James and Mary Fenning. Bond 3 June 1790. Married 26 June
1790 by John Mullins. Sur. and Wit. John Wood. p.36.

PARKER, James and Elizabeth Wilkins. Bond 8 March 1794. Sur. and
Wit. William Powell. p.41.

PARKER, James and Elizabeth Wilkins. Bond 19 May 1794. Sur. and
Wit. William Holt. p.41

PARKER, James, widower, and Miss Lucy Owen, over 21 years. Bond
6 February 1810. Sur. and Wit. John Robinson. p.69.

PARKES, Abel and Elizabeth Degle. Bond 26 July 1852. Sur. and Wit.
Robert Pines. p.142.

PARKS, Abel and Miss Ann Deagle. Bond 4 November 1844. Married
6 November 1844 by George Northam. Sur. and Wit. James Dunlavey
and James D. Sibley. p.126.

PARKS, Arthur and Rachel Harin, of age. Bond 25 June 1830. Married
12 August 1830 by George Northam. Edward Harin, father of Rachel.
Sur. and Wit. Henry Wroten, Richard H. Hart, and Moris Montgomery.
p.104.

PARKS, Curtis and Frances A. Bawl. Bond 29 November 1847. Married
1 December 1847 by George Northam. Sur. and Wit. John Bundick and
Edward Topping. p. 132.

PARRON, John and Lillian H. Clarke. Bond 22 November 1823. John Clarke,
father of Lillian. Sur. and Wit. Philip Montague, Polly Montague,
and William D. Clarke. p.88.

PARRON, Josiah and Miss Catharine A. Parry. Bond 18 February 1833.
Sur. and Wit. Richard H. Street and Catharine M. Parry. p. 111.

PARRON, William and Catharine Cornelius. Bond 28 November 1796. Sur.
and Wit. Thomas Hundley and Will. Wake. p.45.

PARRY, Ira E. and Olivia A. Garrett. Bond 1 January 1850. Margaret
M. Critcher and George Critcher, guardians of Olivia. Sur. and
Wit. Richard C. Lee and Margaret M. Garrett. p.137.

PARRY, Larkin D. and Miss Mary E. Daniel. Bond 17 February 1835.
C. G. Griswold, guardian of Larkin. Robert Daniel, Sr., father of
Mary. Sur. and Wit. John H. Parry and Julia E. Griswold. p.115.

PATTERSON, John and Milley Burton, free people of color. Bond 11 June
1832. Sur. and Wit. John Jefferson and Noah Small. p.108.

PATTERSON, Richard and Elizabeth Kidd. Bond 5 February 1760. William
Kidd, father of Elizabeth. Sur. and Wit. Robert Elliott. p.11.

PATTERSON, Thomas and Elizabeth Batchelder. Bond 23 October 1782. Sur. and Wit. Henry Batchelder. p.26.

PATTERSON, Thomas and Caroline Deaton. Bond 18 February 1840. Married 21 February 1840 by George Northam. Sur. and Wit. John Jefferson. p.120.

PAYNE, Michael and Mary Elliot. Bond 23 March 1773. Elizabeth Elliot, mother of Mary. Sur. and Wit. Benjamin Chew Crockett, Will. Church-hill, and Jno. McNihal. p.17.

PEA, Austin and Fanny Woodford. Bond 1 July 1829. Sur. and Wit. George Healy. p.102.

PEACHY, Thomas Griffin, of Amelia County, and Elizabeth Mills. Bond 22 September 1783. Sur. and Wit. Bennett Browne. p.27.

PEARCE, Robert B. and Sara A. South. Bond 21 May 1849. Married 24 May 1849 by R. A. Christian, with personal consent of father of wife [name not given.] Sur. and Wit. William C. Bassette. p.136.

PEARCE, William D. and Miss Elizabeth Moore. Bond 24 September 1840. Married 24 September 1840 by George Northam. Sur. and Wit. John Lewis. p.121.

PENN, David and Betsey Cloudas, a free mulatto. Bond 14 August 1833. Married 18 August 1833 by George Northam. Sur. and Wit. John Sears. p.111.

PERKS, John and Miss Alcia (or Alice) Dunn. Bond 11 April 1810. Agrippa Dunn, father of Alcia. Sur. and Wit. Dabney A. Miller and B. Kidd. p.70.

PERRIN, William K., Esq., of Gloucester County, and Mrs. Sarah Tayloe Nicolson. Bond 18 December 1833. Married 31 December 1833 by Jno. Cole of Gloucester County. Sur. and Wit. Wyndham Kemp. p. 113.

PERRY, Elisha W. and Mary F. Harrow, widow. Bond 4 November 1850. Sur. and Wit. Robert Dudley and Henry L. Harrow. p.139.

PETERS, William and Henrietta Ridgway. Bond 28 August 1780. Sur. and Wit. John Dungee. p.23.

PITT, Dr. Douglas and Anne Catharine Wortham. Bond 15 January 1850. Married 15 January 1850 by R. A. Christian. Anna F. Wortham, mother of Anne. Sur. and Wit. Benjamin F. Robinson, Martha M. Montague, and James A. Wortham. p.138.

POOL, Dr. Warren W. S. and Miss Amanda Barrick. Bond 23 March 1846. Married 26 March 1846 by George Northam. Sarah Barrick, guardian of Amanda. Sur. and Wit. Andrew Stiff. p.130.

POPE, Elliott and Miss Eliza Healy. Bond 21 October 1834. Sur. and
Wit. James Jones. p.114.

POTTER (PORTER), John R. and Elizabeth Matthews. Bond 23 November
1828. Married 25 November 1828 by George Northam. Sur. and Wit.
W. C. Blake, William Ailworth, and John Woods. p.99.

POTTER, John R. and Miss Arena Vaughan, of lawful age. Bond 21 December 1819. Sur. and Wit. Thomas H. Montague. p.84.

POTTER, John R. and Miss Harriet Armistead, 21 years old. Bond 24 November 1824. Frank Armistead, deceased, father of Harriet. Sur. and
Wit. John G. Anderton, George Northam, and William S. Robinson. p.90.

POWELL, William and Susanna Parker. Bond 4 September 1787. Married
22 September 1787 by Samuel Klug, with consent of David Powell.
Sur. and Wit. Jonathan Herrin. p.31.

POWELL, William and Winefred Gordon, upwards of 30 years of age.
Bond 7 August 1804. Sur. and Wit. Nicholas Wood and John Minter.
p.59.

POWERS, Delaware and Miss Martha Ann Jackson. Bond 28 February 1831.
Married 2 March 1831 by George Northam. Richard Jackson, deceased,
father of Martha. Sur. and Wit. James Shackelford. p.105.

POWERS, James and Susanna Moore. Bond 6 October 1803. Married
8 October 1803 by Argyle W. White, who states James is a widower.
Sur. and Wit. Thomas Bray. p.57.

POWERS, James, of Gloucester County, and Miss Mary Bray. Bond 26 November 1825. Thomas Bray, father of Mary. Sur. and Wit. Enos
Healy. p.93.

PREWIT, Thomas and Ann Shurles. Bond 3 July 1832. Sur. and Wit.
Fielding Shurles. p.109.

PRITCHET, James H. and Mary Christopher. Married 14 March 1838 by
George Northam. [Minister's return only.] p.161.

PRITCHETT, James and Miss Susan A. Montgomery. Married 2 September
1842 by Lewis H. Williams. [Minister's return only.] p.164.

PRITCHETT, Rodham and Mrs. Frances Ware. Bond 12 February 1802.
Robert Ware gives affidavit that Frances was born latter end of
1780. Sur. and Wit. Richard Thruston. p.54.

PRUETT, Thomas R. and Rebecca Dunlavey. Bond 30 May 1839. Married
30 May 1839 by George Northam. Sur. and Wit. John S. Healy. p.118.

QUARLES, John and Elizabeth S. Yates. Bond 9 October 1797. Married
12 October 1797 by Henry Heffernan. Harry B. Yates, father,
Thomas Roane, guardian of Elizabeth. Sur. and Wit. Thomas Churchill,
Carter Berkeley, Rachel Yates, and Christopher Harwood. p.47.

RAINS, Rawleigh and Susannah Wyatt. Bond 25 January 1830. Sur. and
Wit. Robert Mackan, Lewis B. Montague, and Richard H. Street. p.102.

RANDOLPH, Beverley and Miss Agatha Wormeley. Bond 21 January 1742.
Sur. and Wit. Ralph Wormeley, Jno. Price, and Luke Burford. p.1.

READ, Daniel and Miss Susannah B. Batchelder. Bond 8 December 1812.
James Batchelder, deceased, father of Susannah. Sur. and Wit. John
B. Garland. p.75.

READ, Edmund and Lucy Claudus, over 21 years. Bond 29 June 1803. Sur.
and Wit. George Lamkin and Oswald S. Kemp. p.56.

READ, Robert and Miss Nancy Greenwood. Bond 11 November 1812. William
George, guardian of Nancy. Sur. and Wit. William George. p.75.

REVAL, George and Miss Ann Davis. Bond 21 February 1844. Sur. and Wit.
Seth Montgomery and John A. Miles. p.125.

REVEER, George B. and Miss Letitia A. Blake. Bond 31 May 1843. Married
31 May 1843 by George Northam. Sur. and Wit. John B. Blake. p.123.

REVEER, Isaac and Sarah Barrick. Bond 27 December 1802. Married 30 December 1802 by Henry Heffernan. David Barrack, father of Sarah.
Sur. and Wit. William Barrick. p.55.

REVEER, Isaac and Martha Ann Clare. Bond 26 November 1838. Married
29 November 1838 by George Northam. Sur. and Wit. Robert Clare. p.118.

REVEER, James B. and Eleanor H. Woods. Bond 14 June 1848. Married
__ June 1848 by Holland Walker. Sur. and Wit. Richard A. Davis and
Joel Walker. p.134.

REVEER, James B. and Parke Harley Watts. Consent dated 16 August 1852.
Sur. and Wit. Edward Topping. [Consent only.] p.142.

REVEER, Joel and Miss Sarah C. Reveer. Bond 14 April 1845. Married
15 April 1845 by George Northam. Sur. and Wit. Peter Reveer. p.128.

REVEER, Peter and Miss Frances Blake. Bond 14 November 1844. Married
14 November 1844 by George Northam. Sur. and Wit. Joel Walker. p.126.

REVERE, George B. and Lucy Ann Mountain. Bond 7 April 1830. Married
13 April 1830 by George Northam. Sur. and Wit. Robert Mountain.
p.103.

REVIER, Bushrod C. and Miss Nancy Cloughton, who signs own consent. Bond 15 January 1817. William Cloughton, deceased, father of Nancy. Sur. and Wit. John Thomas. p. 81

RHODES, Benjamin and Miss Dorothy Fearn. Bond 21 November 1750. Sur. and Wit. John Wortham. p.5.

RHODES, John and Ann Fearn, widow. Bond 7 November 1745. Sur. and Wit. Chr. Curtis. p.3.

RICHESON, William and Susanna Walden. Bond 3 September 1798. Sur. and Wit. Robert Chowning. p.48.

RIPLEY, Lemuel and Polly Crittenden. Bond 1 March 1800. John Seward,Jr., guardian of Polly. Sur. and Wit. John Seward, Jr. p.51.

RITCHIE, Archibald and Patsey Hipkins Roane. Married 25 July 1797, out of the county, by Henry Heffernan. p.152.

ROANE, James A. and Verlinda L. Clayton. Bond 24 October 1842. Joseph Clayton, guardian of Verlinda. Sur. and Wit. James L. Vaughn and John W. Hughes. p.121.

ROANE, John and Caty Murray. Bond 3 January 1785. Sur. and Wit. William Murray. p.28.

ROANE, Samuel and Miss Ann Frances Woodward. Bond 20 September 1833. Henley Woodward, father of Ann. Sur. and Wit. Henley Woodward. p.111.

ROANE, Thomas and Sally Murray. Bond 26 February 1781. Sur. and Wit. George Lorimer. p.24.

ROANE, William, of Gloucester County, and Sarah Daniel, spinster. Bond 15 February 1754. Sur. and Wit. William Upshaw of Essex County, W. Roane, Jr., and Thomas Price, Jr. p.8.

ROANE, William P. and Mary Susan Bland. Bond 2 July 1849. Married 3 July 1849 by Thomas C. Hayes. Sur. and Wit. Archer Bland. p.136.

ROBINSON, Benjamin and Hannah Churchhill. Bond 1 October 1777. Sur. and Wit. Francis Hargrove. p.21.

ROBINSON, Benjamin F. and Mrs. Eliza. Mountague, Bond 12 October 1825. Eliza. is widow of Thomas H. Montague. Sur. and Wit. Thomas Jones. p.92.

ROBINSON, Benjamin F. [incomplete and not dated.] Sur. and Wit. Jas. Chow. p.143.

ROBINSON, Benjamin F. and Matilda J. Palmer. Married 4 August 1841 by George Northam. [Minister's return only.] p.162.

ROBINSON, Charles and Elizabeth Wood. Married 18 February 1802 by
Henry Heffernan. [Minister's return only.] p.154.

ROBINSON, Christopher and Sarah Wormeley. Bond 4 May 1752. Sur. and
Wit. Christopher Curtis. p.6.

ROBINSON (ROBERSON), Gabriel and Jinney Key. Bond 2 September 1840.
Sur. and Wit. James Key. p.121.

ROBINSON, John, Jr. and Susanna Blake. Bond 30 December 1803. Married 1 January 1804 by Henry Heffernan. John Blake, father of
Susanna. Sur. and Wit. John Blake. p.57.

ROBINSON, Peter and Miss Sarah Lister. Bond 9 August 1750. Edmond
Berkeley, guardian of Sarah. Sur. and Wit. Christopher Robinson
and George Smith. p.5.

ROBINSON, Peter and Nancy Stiff. Bond 17 February 1796. Married
18 February 1796 by Henry Heffernan. William Stiff, father of
Nancy. Sur. and Wit. William Robinson. p.44.

ROBINSON, Peter and Mrs. Mildred Humphries. Bond 30 May 1818. Sur.
and Wit. George D. Nicolson. p.84.

ROBINSON, William and Ann Dunlevy. Bond 9 February 1778. Sur. and
Wit. James Dunlevy. p.22.

ROBINSON, William and Ursala Robinson. Bond 23 August 1784. Sur. and Wit.
Charles Robinson. p.27.

ROBINSON, William and Frances Healy, spinster. Bond 25 February 1799.
Married 28 February 1799 by Henry Heffernan. Sur. and Wit. Peter
Kemp, Jr. p.49.

ROBINSON, William and Miss Betsy Lilly. Bond 12 March 1806. Consent signed Eliza Lilly. Sur. and Wit. Staige Davis, Thomas
Churchill, and Lucy B. Churchill. p.61.

ROBINSON, William and Mrs. Rebecca Bristow. Bond 18 May 1816.
Rebecca widow of James B. Bristow, deceased. Sur. and Wit.
Zachariah Seward. p.81.

ROBINSON, William D. and Mary S. Ward, over 21 years of age. Bond
19 July 1815. Joshua Ward, father, Lydia Ward, mother, of Mary.
Sur. and Wit. Daniel S. Ward. p.79.

ROBINSON, William S. and Miss Alice Blake. Bond 16 November 1826.
Robert N. Blake, father of Alice. Sur. and Wit. Robert N. Blake
and George Healy. p.95.

ROGERS, John and Nancy Ware. Bond 28 September 1795. Robert Ware, father of Nancy, consents. Sur. and Wit. Philip Lee, William Jones, Penelope Lee, and Betsy Brooks. p.43.

ROOTES, John, bachelor, and Miss Sarah Reade. Bond 26 March 1760. Bartholomew Yates gives consent. Sur. and Wit. Phil. Rootes, Leonard Price, and Alex. Dalgleish. p.11.

ROOTES, Philip and Frances Wilcox. Bond 7 December 1756. Sur. and Wit. Richard Corbin and Tho. Shipton. p.9.

ROOTES, Thomas Reade of King and Queen County, and Martha (Jaquelin) Smith. Bond 8 February 1763. John Smith, Esq., father of Martha. Sur. and Wit. Augustine Smith of Gloucester. p.14.

ROSE, Henry and Miss Mary Garland. Bond 27 October 1834. Thomas Rose, father of Henry, consents. John B. Garland, deceased, father of Mary. Sur. and Wit. Paulin A. Blackburn. p.114.

ROSE, Henry and Lucy Ann Major. Bond 29 July 1839. Sur. and Wit. John S. Healy and John W. Palmer. p.119.

ROSE, Isaac and Fanny Jackson, above 21 years. Bond 19 April 1804. Sur. and Wit. Christopher Owen and Leonard Jackson. p.58.

SADLER, Elias R. and Nancy P. Lewis. Bond 12 July 1848. Sur. and Wit. Charles Roane, Jr. and John P. Bristow. p.134.

ST.JOHN, William and Nancy Harwood, above age of 21. Bond 1 September 1803. Sur. and Wit. Christopher Owen and C. Harwood. p.56.

SANDERS, Thomas, (Jr.) and Avarilla Stiff. Bond 26 June 1753. Sur. and Wit. Jacob Stiff and W. Young. p.7.

SANDERS, Thomas and Mary Blackburn, widow. Bond 7 January 1764. Sur. and Wit. Edward Bristow, Sr. and ___ja Wiatt. p. 15.

SAUNDERS, George and Elizabeth Brooks. Bond 31 December 1801. Samuel Brooks, father of Elizabeth. Sur. and Wit. Thomas Montague and John Saunders. p.53.

SAUNDERS, George and Miss Lucy Jones. Bond 27 June 1831. Married 30 June 1831 [the minister's name omitted from return.] Sur. and Wit. John Watts. p.106.

SAUNDERS, George Davis and Charlotte Marchant. Bond 28 December 1790. James Spark gives consent for Charlotte. Sur. and Wit. James Spark. p.36.

SAUNDERS, Jacob Stiff and Lucy Humphries. Bond 11 November 1780. Sur. and Wit. John Humphries. p.24.

SAUNDERS, Jacob S. and Mrs. Dianah Humphries. Bond 16 April 1814.
Dianah,widow of Staige Humphries, deceased. Sur. and Wit. John H.
Saunders. p.77.

SAUNDERS, Jacob and Miss Harriett Williams. Bond 18 February 1835.
Married 26 February 1835 by George Northam. John H. Saunders, father
of Jacob. Sur. and Wit. George T. R. Healy, John Cundiff, W.Harrow,
and Morris Montgomery. p.115.

SAUNDERS, John and Miss Catharine Seward. Bond 6 August 1809. Benjamin
Seward, Sr., deceased, father, Thomas Blake, guardian, of Catharine.
Sur. and Wit. Benjamin Seward and Elizabeth Blake. p.68.

SAUNDERS, Thomas and Mary Stiff. Bond 27 July 1792. Sur. and Wit.
John Humphries, Sr. p.39.

SAUNDERS, Thomas and Elizabeth P. Badley. Bond 16 December 1814. Sur.
and Wit. Jacob Saunders. p.78.

SAYRE, William Samuel and Jane Grymes. Bond 23 July 1804. Married
23 July 1804 by Henry Heffernan. Philip L. Grymes, father of Jane.
Sur. and Wit. Philip L. Grymes. p.59.

SCANLEN, Michael and Emily Bland. Bond 4 March 1850. Father of Emily
consents in person. Sur. and Wit. Archer Bland. p.138.

SCOTT, Delphos and Sarah Faulkner. Bond 28 May 1779. Sur. and Wit.
John Boss and Will. Churchhill. p.23.

SCRATOR, William and Miss Mary Blake. Bond 1 March 1843. Married
1 March 1843 by Richard A. Christian. Sur. and Wit. Benjamin B.
Sibley and Norborn C. Sibley. p.122.

SEARS, Henry and Elizabeth Blackley. Bond 25 February 1799. Sur. and
Wit. Benjamin Jacobs and Peter Kemp, Jr. p.49.

SEARS, Henry and Patsey Jarvis, above 21 years. Bond 20 October 1808.
Sur. and Wit. Thomas Trice. p.67.

SEARS, Henry, widower, and Elizabeth Dunlavey, widow. Bond 27 October
1810. Married 10 November 1810 by Philip Montague. Sur. and Wit.
John Seward. p.71.

SEARS, Henry and Miss Nancy Watts. Bond 9 November 1825. Ralph Watts,
father of Nancy. Sur. and Wit. Thomas Hundley, Jr. p.93.

SEARS, Henry and Miss Jane Walden. Bond 1 January 1829. Sur. and Wit.
John Walden. p.100.

SEARS, Henry and Miry Ann Edwards. Bond 20 November 1849. Married
___ November 1849 by Thomas B. Evans. Sur. and Wit. Thomas C.
Edwards. p.137.

SEARS, John and Polly Kidd. Bond 28 April 1806. Henry Kidd, deceased, father, John Sears, guardian, of Polly. Sur. and Wit. Henry Thurston. p.62.

SEARS, John and Lucy Mickelborough, free woman of color. Bond 1 June 1832. Sur. and Wit. George Healy. p.108.

SEARS, Philip and Eleanor Goode. Bond 26 September 1791. Married 29 September 1791 by John Mullins. Sur. and Wit. John Thruston. p.37.

SEARS, Thomas and Catey Collier. Married 1 August 1799 by Henry Heffernan. [Minister's return only.] p.153.

SEBREE, Nicholas and Betsa Barnes. Bond 14 June 1796. Married 15 June 1796 by Henry Heffernan. Sur. and Wit. Amos Faulkner and Peggy Mason. p.45.

SEGAR, Cyrus and Maria E. D. Foster. Bond 22 December 1830. Sur. and Wit. Lewis B. Montague. p.104.

SEGAR, John and Miss Priscilla Hackney. Bond 17 December 1764. Sur. and Wit. Thomas Segar and William Bickham. p.15.

SEGAR, Richard M. and Miss Polly Roane. Bond 16 January 1812. Thomas Roane, deceased, father of Polly. Sur. and Wit. George Healy. p.73.

SEGAR, William and Nancy Roane. Bond 16 September 1791. Sur. and Wit. Staige Davis. p.37.

SEGAR, William and Penelope Montague. Bond 22 September 1801. Sur. and Wit. Elliott Muse, Thomas Montague, and Philip Montague. p.53.

SEWARD, Benjamin and Miss Mary Saunders, of age. Bond 25 September 1807. Sur. and Wit. Thomas Blake. p.65.

SEWARD, Edward and Avey Southern. Bond 24 August 1789. Sur. and Wit. John Seward, Peter Kemp, Jr., and William Segar. p.34.

SEWARD, Edward S. and Lucy Ann B. Seward. Bond 22 December 1828. John Seward, deceased, father of Lucy. Sur. and Wit. Edward Seward. p.100.

SEWARD, James and Nancy Seward. Bond 31 December 1801. Zachariah Seward, father; Thomas Cook, uncle, of James. Benjamin Seward, father of Nancy. Sur. and Wit. Edmond Simcoe, Lewis Seward, Charles Lee, and Zachariah Seward. p.53.

SEWARD, James T. of King and Queen County and Frances E. Corr. Bond 24 September 1850. Married __ September 1850 by Thomas B. Evans. Sur. and Wit. Thomas Corr, Perry M. Peckham, Jr. p. 139.

SEWARD, John (Jack) and [Mary Shepherd.] Bond 23 January 1797. Married
2 February 1797 by Henry Heffernan. The wife's name does not appear
on bond, but is written into marriage register and in minister's
return. Sur. and Wit. Edward Seward and Agrippa Dunn. p.46.

SEWARD, John and Miss Jane Dudley, age 21. Bond 15 April 1807. Sur.
and Wit. Edward Seward, Thomas Street, and William M. Burke. p.64.

SEWARD, John, Jr. and Susanna Seward. Bond 7 May 1803. Benjamin Seward,
father of Susanna. Sur. and Wit. William Sinko, Thomas Oliver, and
Garrett Daniel. p.56.

SEWARD, John, Sr. and Mary Mickelburough, widow. Bond 25 July 1803.
Sur. and Wit. William Simcoe, Jr., J. Chew, Jr., and Thomas Kidd.
p.56.

SEWARD, John E. and Frances J. Trice. Bond 26 January 1847. Married
28 January 1847 by George Northam. Sur. and Wit. Lewis B. Seward
and Mary Trice. p.131.

SEWARD, John E. and Martha M. Didlake. Bond 5 August 1851. Married
5 August 1851 by Zach. Street. Sur. and Wit. Lewis B. Seward. p.140.

SEWARD, Leroy and Ann Kemp. Bond 14 March 1840. Sur. and Wit. Henry
Sears. p.120.

SEWARD, Lewis and Miss Catharine Montague. Bond 2 October 1833. Sur.
and Wit. John Puller, Leroy Cauthorn, and Virginia V. Cauthorn. p.112.

SEWARD, Lewis B. and Miss Sarah Garrett. Bond 27 February 1832. Sur.
and Wit. George Garrett. p.107.

SEWARD, Lewis B. and Miss Catharine C. Trice. Bond 27 May 1844. Married
29 May 1844 by George W. Trice. Sur. and Wit. Robert N. Trice and
Frances J. Trice. p.125.

SEWARD, W. W. [not dated and incomplete.] Sur. and Wit. Edward
Seward. p.143.

SHACKELFORD, George D. and Martha C. Lewis, of age and signs own consent. Bond 13 October 1817. Iverson Lewis, deceased, father. Sur.
and Wit. Thomas G. Crittenden. p.83.

SHACKELFORD, James U. and Miss Lucy Kidd. Bond 14 January 1830.
Thomas Kidd, deceased, father of Lucy. Sur. and Wit. Robert
Blakey. p.102.

SHACKELFORD, William D. and Eliza T. Daniel. Bond 19 November 1805.
Lydia Daniel, mother and guardian of Eliza. Sur. and Wit. Lydia
Daniel and John Jesse. p.60.

SHAKELFORD, Edwin and Francis Good(e). Bond 22 February 1838. Thomas
Goode, father of Francis. Sur. and Wit. Thomas Goode. p.117.

SHARROD, John and Susan Greenwood. Married 14 March 1841 by George
Northam. [Minister's return only.] p.162.

SHEPARD, Henry and Mary Daniel. Bond 3 November 1760. Mary is widow
of George Daniel, deceased. Sur. and Wit. Henry Shepard, Sr. and
Philip Mountague. p.12.

SHEPHERD, George D. and Eunice B. Chowning. Bond 26 October 1795.
Married 21 November 1795 by Henry Heffernan. Sur. and Wit.
Churchill Blakey and Thomas Muse, Jr. p.43.

SHEPHERD, Henry D. and Mary Daniel. Bond 15 December 1789. Married
19 December 1789 by Samuel Klug. Sur. and Wit. Nelson Daniel. p.35.

SHEPHERD, Jeremiah and Esther Daniel. Bond 8 May 1756. Sur. and Wit.
Henry Shepherd, Braxton Bird, and Thomas Price. p.9.

SHEPHERD, William and Miss Lucy Woodward. Bond 5 September 1821.
Philemon Woodward, father of Lucy. Sur. and Wit. Philemon Woodward.
p.85.

SHEPHERD, William and Miss Isabella R. Woodward. Bond 3 September 1827.
Married 6 September 1827 by Richard Claybrook who shows William's
name with the title Colonel. Richard Woodward, father of Isabella.
Sur. and Wit. Richard Woodward. p.98.

SHIPLEY, Elisha and Miss Susan Dobson. Bond 18 January 1827. Marha
Dobson, parent of Susan. Sur. and Wit. William Dobson and James
Jones. p.96.

SHIPLEY, Robert and Sarah Dunn. Bond 25 December 1804. Agrippa Dunn,
father of Sarah. Sur. and Wit. Samuel Ware and Samuel Shipley. p.59.

SHIPLEY, Samuel and Nancy Dunn. Bond 23 February 1804. Agrippa Dunn,
father of Nancy. Sur. and Wit. Samuel Ware. p.58.

SHURLDS, Fielding and Mrs. Frances Clear. Bond 1 March 1837. Sur. and
Wit. Thomas J. Palmer and F. Blackburn. p.116.

SIBBLEE, Benjamin and Judith Daniel. Bond 19 July 1794. Sur. and
Wit. Joseph Boss. p.42.

SIBBLEE, Thomas and Mary Layton. Bond 2 May 1791. Sur. and Wit.
Benson Sibblee. p.37.

SIBLEE, Daniel Ball and Nancy Davis Miller. Married 2 June 1796.
by Henry Heffernan. [Minister's return only.] p.151.

SIBLEY, Benjamin B. and Miss Louisa Clarke. Bond 26 July 1840. Married 4 August 1840 by George Northam. John Daniel swears both are of age. Sur. and Wit. John P. Chrispenn. p.120.

SIBLEY, Benjamin B. and Elenor Todd, "more than 21 years". Bond 22 August 1850. Married 26 August 1850 by R. A. Christian. Sur. and Wit. Alfred Palmer, Elizabeth Bell, and B. A. Blake. p.139.

SIBLEY, Daniel and Juliann Blake. Bond 26 March 1827. Sur. and Wit. James U. Wood. p.97.

SIBLEY, Daniel and Mary Parker, "free woman, 21 years old." Bond 4 March 1845. Married 5 March 1845 by Richard A. Christian. Sur. and Wit. Jacob S. Blake and B. B. Sibley. p.127.

SIBLEY, Daniel B. and Mrs. Elizabeth Clarke. Bond 23 April 1817. Elizabeth is widow of Robert Clarke, deceased. Sur. and Wit. John B. Roane. p.82.

SIBLEY, Daniel B., Jr. and Sarah Miller. Bond 28 June 1847. Married 28 June 1847 by R. A. Christian. B. B. Sibley, guardian of Daniel. Sur. and Wit. George B. Daniel. p.132.

SIBLEY, John and Ann Barrick. Bond 28 October 1802. Married 4 November 1802 by Henry Heffernan. Sur. and Wit. David Barrick and Francis West. p.55.

SIBLEY, John D. and Miss Catharine Adkinson. Bond 26 December 1825. Catharine's name is shown as Adkins on consent. Sur. and Wit. Thomas D. Blake and Elizabeth Sibley. p.93.

SIBLEY, Norborn C. and Miss Mary Long. Bond 27 February 1843. Sur. and Wit. John W. Daniel and George W. Barrick. p.122.

SIBLEY, William James, age 25 years, and Martha Ellen Groom, age 21 years, both single. Married 15 February 1854 by Holland Walker at George B. Daniel's. Daniel and Julia Sibley, parents of William, born in Middlesex County. Martha is the daughter of _____Groom and Elizabeth, his wife. [Minister's return only.] p.170.

SIMCO, James H. and Nancy Kidd. Married __ September 1841 by Thomas B. Evans. [Minister's return only.] p.165.

SIMCO, William and Jane Beamon. Bond 1 February 1804. Sur. and Wit. John Clark, Jr. and Rebekah Beamon. p.57.

SIMCOE, Absalom and Miss Mary Howard. Bond 11 October 1808. Sur. and Wit. Robert Palmer. p.66.

SIMCOE, William and Nancey Stevens. Bond 26 November 1792. Married 26 December 1792 by John Mullins. John and Mary Stevens, parents of Nancey, who was born the 4th day of November 1774. Sur. and Wit. Beverley Cloudas. p.39.

SIMCOE, William, Jr., and Lucy Wortham, widow. Bond 14 February 1805. Sur. and Wit. Christopher Owen and Sarah C. Bristow. p.60.

SIMCOE, William and Mary Ann Baker. Bond 13 June 1837. Sur. and Wit. William Baker and Robert Trice. p.117.

SINCLAIR, Arthur and Susannah Phillips, spinster. Bond 22 February 1766. Sur. and Wit. Ja. Gregorie. p.17.

SINETH, Joseph and Mrs. Mary Small. Bond 31 October 1750. Sur. and Wit. William Eastwood and Beverley Stanard. p.5.

SKELTON, Reuben and Elizabeth Lomax. Bond 9 July 1751. Lunsford Lomax, father of Elizabeth. Sur. and Wit. John Robinson, John Price, Abraham Willson, and John Dix. p.6.

SKINNER, Philemon and Melvina L. Beazley. Bond 18 July 1850. John Beazley, father of Melvina. Sur. and Wit. John Beazley and John Beazley [2], p.139.

SLAUGHTER, Richeson and Ann F. Walker. Bond 17 October 1840. Married 29 October 1840 by George Northam. Sur. and Wit. Andrew Stiff and P. H. Fitzhugh. p.121.

SMITH, Cary and Ann Wortham. Bond 24 November 1741. Sur. and Wit. John Wortham and Robert Dudley. p. 1.

SMITH, Francis and Caroline A. Woodward. Bond 29 December 1824. Henley Woodward, Esq., father of Caroline. Sur. and Wit. Henley Woodward. p.91.

SMITH, George W. and Miss Harriet J. Major. Bond 23 April 1831. John A. Major, father of Harriet. Sur. and Wit. Robert C. Garland. p.105.

SMITH, George W. and Mrs. Ann F. Roane. Bond 19 July 1844. Married 24 July 1844 by George Northam. Sur. and Wit. Thomas H. Woodward. p. 126.

SMITH, James and Kitty Hardee. Bond 16 May 1793. Sur. and Wit. William Kidd. p.40.

SMITH, James M. and Miss Virginia A. Thomas. Bond 26 December 1851. Married 30 December 1851 by Holland Walker. M.J.M.Walker, guardian. Sur. and Wit. Edward Topping and John W. Mears. p.141.

SMITH, John R. and Miss Sarah S. Barrick. Bond 6 June 1832. Bailey Barrick, father of Sarah. Sur. and Wit. Bailey Barrick. p.108.

SMITH, John R. and Fanny M. Stiff. Bond 17 December 1819. Sur. and Wit. John Wood. p.84.

SMITH, Maurice and Catherine Jones. Bond 14 May 1753. Sur. and Wit. William Eastham and George Medlicott. p.7.

SMITH, William and Miss Polley M. Major. Bond 24 March 1827. John A. Major, father of Polley. Sur. and Wit. John A. Major. p.96.

SMITHER, Joseph E. and Lucy C. L. Hoskins. Bond 20 December 1848. Married 22 December 1848 by R. A. Christian. Sur. and Wit. William W. Stone and Wiley Wright. p.135.

SMITHER, Thomas and Lucy E. Humphries. Bond 10 March 1828. Married 8 April 1828 by George Northam. Seaton Humphries, deceased, father of Lucy. Sur. and Wit. Carter Purkins, Edm^d Stiff, and Augusteen C. Humphries. p.99.

SOUTH, Hugh A. and Julia Ann E. Bland. Bond 3 August 1850. Married 5 August 1850 by Holland Walker. Thomas J. Bland, father of Julia. Sur. and Wit. Thomas J. Lewis. p.139.

SOUTH, James M. and Sarah Dunlavy. Bond 1 December 1847. Married 1 December 1847 by R. A. Christian. Sur. and Wit. Thomas J. Bland and Thomas J. Lewis. p.133.

SOUTH, James M. and Catharine Haynes. Bond 18 April 1850. Married 18 April 1850 by R. A. Christian. Nancy Haynes, mother of Catharine. Sur. and Wit. Thomas R. Sutton, Frances South, and Rebecca Newbill. p. 138.

SOUTH, Joseph V. and Malissa C. Edwards. Bond 6 January 1846. Married __ January 1846 by John J. Boss. Sur. and Wit. John J. Wake, Elizabeth D. Wood, and John T. Wood. p.130.

SOUTH, Lodewick and Miss Frances Lewis. Bond 23 February 1830. Sur. and Wit. William Lewis. p.103.

SOUTH, William and Judith Williams. Bond 5 November 1791. Married 7 November 1791 by John Mullins. Sur. and Wit. James Wilkins. p.37.

SOUTH, William and Elizabeth Allen. Bond 16 June 1795. Married 18 June 1795 by Robert Ware. Sur. and Wit. George Atkinson. p.42.

SOUTH, William and Miss Sally Moore. Bond 26 November 1821. George Moore, father of Sally. Sur. and Wit. George Moore and James Stamper. p.85.

SOUTH, William and Mrs. Dalinda Garland. Bond 29 December 1832. Sur. and Wit. Robert Mountain. p.110.

SOUTHALL, Philip, of the City of Richmond, and Jane (Jean) Neilson. Bond 12 September 1788. Married 14 September 1788 by Samuel Klug. W. Foushee, City of Richmond, guardian of Jane. Sur. and Wit. John Curtis. p.33.

SPANN, Richard and Miss Priscilla Churchhill, daughter of A. Churchhill, who consents. James Gordon gives his consent for Richard Spann to marry Priscilla Churchhill. Bond 29 December 1759. Sur. and Wit. Armistead Churchill, Jr., Mary Gordon, Braxton Bird, and Richard Chichester. p.11.

SPENCER, Gideon and A. H. Claybrook. Bond 21 October 1828. Richard Claybrook, father of the bride. Sur. and Wit. Thomas B. Evans. p.99.

SPENCER, John and Molly Cooke. Married 7 February 1799 by Henry Heffernan. [Minister's return only.] p.153.

SPENCER, Thomas, Jr. and Miss Mary Meacham. Bond 8 September 1763. John Meacham, father of Mary. Sur. and Wit. William Meacham and John Yarrington. p.15.

SPRATT, Robert and Anne Yates, widow. Bond 16 September 1772. Sur. and Wit. Ja. Gregorie and Zach. Shachelford. p.17.

STAMPER, James and Catharine Jackson. Bond 19 March 1796. Married 20 March 1796 by Henry Heffernan. Sur. and Wit. Thomas Churchill. p.44.

STAMPER, Nelson and Elizabeth Meacham. Bond 12 January 1803. Sur. and Wit. Peter Kemp, Jr. and Jane Meacham. p.55.

STAMPER, Samuel and Sally Kidd. Bond 3 April 1801. Married 4 April 1801 by Henry Heffernan. Sur. and Wit. Thomas Kidd. p.52.

STAND, Henry and Miss Mary Dudley. Bond 15 January 1820. Sur. and Wit. Robert Dudley. p.84.

STANDARD, James S. and Frances Batchelder. Bond 27 January 1807. Married 31 January 1807 by David Corey. "I do hereby certify that from an old family book which did belong to Henry Batchelder and now in my possession that the age of Frances Batchelder, daughter of said Henry, is entered in said book in her father's handwriting in the following words: 'Frances Batchelder, daughter of Henry and Elizabeth, his wife, was born February 7, 1785' Signed, Thomas Healy." Sur. and Wit. James Healy, Jr. and W. J. Ward. p.63.

STEPTOE, William, Esq., and Elizabeth Robinson. Bond 15 May 1782. Christopher Robinson, deceased, father of Elizabeth. Ralph Wormeley, Jr., gives consent. Sur. and Wit. Ralph Wormeley, Jr. p.25.

STEVENS, Edmond (Edmund) and Elizabeth Jesse. Bond 30 December 1800. William Jesse, deceased, father, and John Jesse, guardian, of Elizabeth. Sur. and Wit. John Jesse, Jr. and Richard Jesse. p.52.

STEVENS, James W. and Miss Catherine Owen. Bond 8 August 1816. Mr. Christopher Owen, father of Catherine. Sur. and Wit. Christopher Owen. p.81.

STEVENS, Joseph, of Caroline County, and Anne Wortham. Bond 4 December 1758. Sur. and Wit. George Fearn and Philip Mountague. p.10.

STEWARD, William and Rhoda Gordon, of age. Bond 22 June 1807. Sur. and Wit. Major Wiatt. p.64.

STEWART, William and Nancy Dunn. Bond 22 December 1823. Peachy Dunn, father of Nancy. Sur. and Wit. Lewis Hundley and John Downly. p.89.

STIFF, Andrew and Miss Elizabeth Barrick. Bond 19 December 1843. Married 21 December 1843 by George Northam. Sarah C. Barrick, mother and guardian of Elizabeth. Sur. and Wit. William H. Purkins, H. D. Barrick, and Robert Clare. p.124.

STIFF, Edmond and Miss Polly Humphries. Bond 8 August 1826. Robert Barrick, guardian of Polly. Sur. and Wit. James Stamper, Sarah Barrick, and John Barrick. p.95.

STIFF, Jacob and Mrs. Mary Meacham, widow. Bond 7 September 1743. Sur. and Wit. John Meacham and Luke Burford. p.2.

STIFF, Jacob and Catherine Batchelder, widow. Bond 5 January 1746. Sur. and Wit. Samuel Batchelder, Lewis Mountague, and Richard Major. p.3.

STIFF, James and Betty Blake. 15 December 1774. Sur. and Wit. John Blake. p.20.

STIFF, James and Susanna Wood. Bond 15 March 1796. Married 17 March 1796 by Henry Heffernan. Sur. and Wit. William Wood. p.44.

STIFF, James W. and Louisa Lee. Bond 28 January 1831. Married 1 February 1831 by George Northam. Lewis Lee, deceased, father, and Hiram Walker, guardian,of Louisa. Sur. and Wit. William Stiff and Edmund Stiff. p.105.

STIFF, John and Elizabeth Miller. Bond 23 April 1787. Married 26 April 1787 by Samuel Klug. Sur. and Wit. John Thruston. p.31.

STIFF, John and Catharine E. Barrick. Bond 31 January 1835. Married 3 February 1835 by George Northam. Sur. and Wit. Bailey Barrick. p. 115.

STIFF, John B. and Lucy Sibley (Siblee), under age. Bond 29 December 1800. Married 3 January 1801 by Henry Heffernan. Benson Siblee, father of Lucy. Sur. and Wit. Robert Wake, Daniel B. Siblee, and John Sibley. p.52.

STIFF, Lewis L. and Mary J. Wood. Bond 24 September 1838. Married 26 September 1838 by George Northam. Sur. and Wit. Erastus T. Mountague. p.117.

STIFF, Robert and Miss A.M.F. Palmer. Bond 18 January 1845. Married 19 January 1845 by Richard A. Christian. Henry C. Palmer, father of bride. Sur. and Wit. Richard A. Christian, Jr. and Thomas Muse. p.127.

STIFF, Thomas H. and Elizabeth B. Bennet. Married 7 September 1837 by George Northam. [Minister's return only.] p.161.

STIFF, William and Sarah Meacham. Bond 3 September 1751. James Meacham, deceased, father of Sarah. Sur. and Wit. William Meacham and William Segar. p.6.

STIFF, William and Nancy Palmer. Married 9 June 1842 by George Northam. [Minister's return only.] p.162.

STIFF, William Nelson and Sarah Healy. Bond 25 January 1796. Married 28 January 1796 by Henry Heffernan. Thomas Healy, father of Sarah. Sur. and Wit. Peter Robinson and Charles Curtis. p.44.

STIFFE, Tom and Elizabeth Davis. Married 20 February 1796 by Henry Heffernan. [Minister's return only.] p.151.

STONE, Richard and Miss Polly Clarke. Bond 25 August 1817. Sur. and Wit. John Clarke. p. 83.

STREET, Henry and Lucy Chowning. Bond 12 January 1786. Sur. and Wit. John Daniel. p.29.

STREET, John and Frances Clarke. Bond 27 October 1806. Sur. and Wit. John Clarke, Jr. p.63.

STREET, John and Mary F. Daniel. Bond 27 March 1848. Issued by personal consent of father of wife. Sur. and Wit. Mickelborough Daniel. p.133.

STREET, Thomas and Miss Ann Owen. Bond 14 December 1809. Christopher Owen, father of Ann. Sur. and Wit. Christopher Owen. p.68.

STREET, Thomas and Elizabeth D. Stiff. Bond 9 February 1829. Married 10 February 1829 by George Northam. Sur. and Wit. William Jesse, John Chowning, Jr., and Willantina Robinson. p.101.

STREET, Zachariah and Ursula Lee. Bond 24 March 1834. Sur. and Wit. Lewis B. Montague. p.113.

STRINGER, Daniel and Miss Ursula Laughlin. Bond 6 April 1765. Sur. and Wit. John Batcheldor. p.16.

SULLIVAN, Francis and Mrs. Mary Powers. Bond 19 December 1843. Married 20 December 1843 by Richard A. Christian. Sur. and Wit. Enos Healy. p. 124.

SUMMERSON (SOMERSON), John and Mary Gaines. Bond 15 December 1834. Sur. and Wit. Joseph Clarkson. p.114.

SUTTON, John Gayle and Ann Wake. Bond 8 June 1791. Sur. and Wit. John Wake and Christopher Robinson. p.37.

SUTTON, Rowland and Ann Morgan. Bond 7 May 1751. Sur. and Wit. William Morgan. p.6.

SUTTON, Thomas R. and Martha Ann Beazeley. Bond 24 December 1839. Married 26 December 1839 by George Northam. Sur. and Wit. James W. Games and John Beazeley. p.119.

SUTON (or TUTON),Thomas and Ann E. Robinson. Bond 24 December 1849. Married 26 December 1849 by Holland Walker. Sur. and Wit. Benjamin F. Robinson. p. 137.

SWORD, Edward and Avey Southern. Married 27 August 1789 by John Mullins. [Minister's return only.] p.149.

SWORD, John and Jane Dudley. Married 16 April 1807 by David Corey. [Minister's return only.] p.155.

SYMMER, John and Hannah Potter, widow. Bond 12 January 1749. Sur. and Wit. Robert Page. p.5.

TAFF, Thomas and Miss Lucy A. Greenwood. Bond 5 November 1832. Sur. and Wit. William D. Clarke and Edwin Greenwood. p.109.

TANKERSLEY, Thornley B. and Miss Priscilla Todd. Bond 24 December 1824. Benjamin Todd, father of Priscilla. Sur. and Wit. Joseph Todd. p.90.

TAYLOE, John, Jr., of Richmond County, and Miss Rebecca Plator. Bond 21 May 1747. George Plator, Esq. of St. Marys County, Maryland, father of Rebecca. Sur. and Wit. Richard Corbin of King & Queen County, and Richard Barnes. p.4.

TAYLOR, Eli and Elizabeth Dudley, spinster. Bond 30 April 1799. Married 4 May 1799 by Henry Heffernan. Consent of Ann Dudley, mother of Elizabeth. Sur. and Wit. James Hopkins and Robert Mickelburrough. p.50.

TAYLOR, John and Elizabeth Blakey, widow. Bond 2 June 1760. Sur. and Wit. John Yarrington. p.12.

TAYLOR, John and Ann Rogers. Bond 6 October 1762. Sur. and Wit. John Yarrington and Edmond Mickelburrough. p.13.

TAYLOR, Dr. John R. and Willantina Robinson. Bond 17 June 1829. Married 17 June 1829 by George Northam. Sur. and Wit. R. A. Christian, E. D. Street, and Lucia S. Stiff. p.101.

TAYLOR, Richard and Mrs. Maria Lee. Bond 26 March 1823. Maria is
widow of Archelas Lee, deceased. Sur. and Wit. Mickelborough
Daniel and Charle G. Layton. p.87.

TAYLOR, William and Priscilla Segar. Bond 11 May 1775. Sur. and Wit.
Daniel Dejarnett and Philip Mountague. p.20.

TEMPLE, Benjamin, Jr. and Miss Lucy L. Robinson. Bond 25 September
1826. Married 26 September 1826 by Richard Claybrook. John
Chowning, Jr., guardian of Lucy. Sur. and Wit. John Chowning, Jr.
and W. H. Roy. p.95.

TENOE, Stephen and Ann Rhodes. Bond 17 December 1744. John Rhodes
(at Urbanner) father of Ann. Sur. and Wit. Robert Price and A.
Frazier. p.3.

THOMAS, George of Hanover County, bachelor, and Dorothy Elliott. Bond
7 August 1758. Henry Whiting, guardian of Dorothy. Sur. and Wit.
Henry Whiting, William Moulson, Mary Moulson, John Gordon, and
Stanton Dudley. p.10.

THOMAS, George and Miss Judith Mercer. Bond 13 May 1826. Sur. and Wit.
John Chowning, Jr. p.94.

THOMAS, John and Miss Hannah Knight. Bond 7 November 1809. John Knight,
father, and Francis Walker, guardian, of Hannah. Sur. and Wit.
Nelson Humphries and George Revier. p.68.

THORNTON, Francis and Elizabeth Hackney. Bond 17 December 1782. Sur.
and Wit. Benjamin Hackney. p.26.

THORNTON, Francis, Jr. and Miss Maria Hackney. Bond 21 August 1807.
Benjamin Hackney, father of Maria. Sur. and Wit. Benjamin Hackney.
p.64.

THORNTON, Francis, Sr., of Gloucester County, and Miss Elizabeth L.
Hackney. Bond 2 September 1807. Sur. and Wit. Benjamin Hackney
and Francis Thornton, Jr. p.64.

THRIFT, Robert T. and Elizabeth Ware. Bond 27 September 1840. Sur.
and Wit. Lewis B. Seward. p.121.

THRUSTON, Henry and Elizabeth Clark. Bond 26 September 1791. Married
6 October 1791 by John Mullins. Sur. and Wit. Philip Sears. p.37.

THRUSTON, William and Mary Smith. Bond 12 April 1793. Sur. and Wit.
William Kidd. p.40.

THURSTON, Batchelder and Peggy Daniel. Bond 27 February 1786. Sur.
and Wit. William Thurston. p.30.

THURSTON, James H. and Martha A. Trice. Married __ October 1841, by
Thomas B. Evans. [Minister's return only.] p.165.

THURSTON, John and Polly Dunn. Bond 17 June 1795. Agrippa Dunn, father of Polly, consents. Sur. and Wit. Newbill Dunn and Catherine Dunn. p.42.

THURSTON, John and Elizabeth Richeson, spinster, of age. Bond 18 December 1801. Affidavit of William George, Jr., uncle of Elizabeth. Sur. and Wit. John Jesse and Overton Cosby. p.53.

THURSTON, John S. and Sally Daniel. Bond 3 July 1810. Travis Daniel, deceased, father, and Burgess Kidd, guardian, of Sally. Sur. and Wit. Burgess Kidd. p.70.

THURSTON, Robert and Constant Daniel. Bond 2 June 1742. Sur. and Wit. Richard Allen, Richard Pattison, and Thomas Price. p. 1.

THURSTON, Robert and Margaret Jones, spinster. Bond 26 October 1765. Sur. and Wit. John George, Jr. and Elizabeth George. p.16.

THURSTON, Thacker and Miss Nancy K. Cundiff. Bond 26 January 1837. Married 26 January 1837 by George Northam. Sur. and Wit. Alfred Healy and Lucy B. D. Sutton. p.116.

THURSTON, William and Sally Crossfield, single, above 21 years. Bond 2 January 1806. James Crossfield, brother of Sally. Sur. and Wit. James Crossfield and Samuel Coke. p.61.

THURSTON, William and Mary Smith. Married 13 April 1793 by John Mullins. [Minister's return only.] p.150.

TODD, Benjamin and Miss Eliza Harrow, from 25 to 26 years old. Bond 26 October 1831. Married 27 October 1831 by George Northam. William Harrow, father of Eliza. Sur. and Wit. Zachariah U. Crittenden and Catherine C. Crittenden. p.106.

TODD, John T. and Miss Eleanor Blake. Bond 31 January 1844. Married 1 February 1844 by George Northam. W. C. Blake, father of Eleanor. Sur. and Wit. John L. Blake. p.125.

TODD, Joseph and Martha Green. Bond 20 December 1831. Married 22 December 1831 by George Northam. Sur. and Wit. T. B. Tankersley and William Green. p.107.

TOMLINSON, William and Lucy Hackney. Bond 25 November 1805. William Hackney, father and David Corey, guardian, of Lucy. Sur. and Wit. David Corey. p.60.

TOOL, Garret and Elizabeth Saunders. Bond 11 October 1793. Sur. and Wit. David Garland. p.40.

TOWELL, Mark W., of Lancaster County, and Miss Elizabeth Elliott Pace. Bond 16 March 1832. John Merideth of Lancaster County, guardian, and consents for Mark. George S. Pace, father of Elizabeth. Sur. and Wit. Robert Barrick, William Gresham, and William Pace. p.108.

TOWNES, Richard and Eliz^a Burk. Bond 23 January 1753. Sur. and Wit.
Henry Thacker and William Allen. p.7.

TRADER, George and Miss Patsey Deagle, of age. Bond 23 April 1807.
Married 26 April 1807 by David Corey. Sur. and Wit. David Corey.
p.64.

TRADER, George and Miss Amelia Hart. Bond 9 January 1833. Richard
Hart, deceased, father and Susan Hart, mother of Amelia. Sur. and
Wit. William Norton. p.111.

TRADER, James and Susan A. Sharrod. Bond 15 December 1847. Sur. and
Wit. Bartlett Davis and R. H. Crittenden. p.133.

TRADER, Levi and Parmelia Trader. Bond 11 January 1851. Sur. and Wit.
Hiram Deagle and James Pritchett. p.140.

TRADER, William and Miss Priscilla Fitzgerald. Bond 25 September 1832.
Eliza Fitzgerald, mother of Priscilla. Sur. and Wit. Thomas
Fitzgerald. p. 109.

TRICE, James and Frances Lee. Bond 9 July 1795. Sur. and Wit. George
Fallis. p.43.

TRICE, James and Miss Catharine Watts. Bond 15 August 1827. Married
15 August 1827 by Richard Claybrook. Sur. and Wit. Leroy H. Trice.
p.97.

TRICE, Leroy H. and Ann J. Ware. Bond 9 October 1828. Samuel Ware,
father of Ann. Sur. and Wit. Robert Daniel, Jr. p.98.

TRICE, Robert and Miss Elizabeth Lee. Bond 3 January 1825. Married
3 January 1825 by Richard Claybrook. Sur. and Wit. James Stamper
and Thomas Trice, Jr. p.91.

TRICE, Thomas, Jr. and Miss Mary Ann Kidd. Bond 22 December 1824.
Married 24 December 1824 by Richard Claybrook. Thomas Kidd, deceased, father of Mary Ann. Sur. and Wit. Robert Blakey. p.90.

TRICE, Captain Thomas.and Ann H. Lee. Bond 13 April 1839. Sur. and
Wit. Robert Trice and Elizabeth Trice. p.118.

TRICE, Captain Thomas and Jane W. Blackley. Bond 26 July 1840. Married 26 July 1840 by Richard A. Christian. Sur. and Wit. John W.
Palmer, Louisa M. Muse, and William Wortham. p.120.

TUGGLE, Griffin and Frances Berry. Bond 2 January 1779. Sur. and
Wit. Nicholas Tuggle. p.22.

TUGGLE, Griffin and Patsey Dillard. Bond 2 September 1800. George
Dillard, father of Patsey. Sur. and Wit. George Dillard. p.51.

TUGGLE, Lodowick and Dorothy Lee, spinster. Bond 1 October 1765.
Sur. and Wit. John George and John Stringer. p.16.

TURBERVILLE, George Lee and Betty Tayloe Corbin. .Bond 24 June 1782.
Richard Corbin, grandfather of Betty, consents. Sur. and Wit.
Robert Spratt, John Tayloe Corbin, and G. C. Tucker. p.25.

TURNER, Major and Sally Daniel. Bond 28 March 1796. Sur. and Wit.
Philip Lee. p.45.

TURNER, William D. of Gloucester County, and Miss Louisa C. Barrick,
of the age of twenty-one. Bond 23 December 1831. Married 24 December 1831 by George Northam. Sur. and Wit. George W. Palmer,
James Barrick, and Catharine E. Barrick. p.107.

UPSHAW, Edwin and Lucy Roane. Married 25 May 1800 by Henry Heffernan.
[Minister's return only.] p.153.

USERY (USSERY), Thomas of Essex County, and Jane Cornelius. Bond
24 May 1799. Mary Ann Cornelius, Hannah Cornelius, aunts of Jane,
give consent. Sur. and Wit. Lewis Montague and Peter Kemp, Jr. p.50.

VALENTINE, Jacob, of King William County, and Elizabeth Batcheldor.
Bond 29 September 1762. Elizabeth, widow of Samuel Batchelder, deceased. Sur. and Wit. Simon Laughlin and William Bickham. p.13.

VASS, Henry and Catharine Turner. Bond 24 January 1774. Sur. and Wit.
Philip Mountague and Jasper Clayton. p. 19.

VASS, Henry and Elizabeth Pryor. Bond 22 November 1779. Sur. and Wit.
William Pryor. p.23.

VASS, Vincent of Essex County, and Jane Mountague, widow. Bond 22
August 1757. Sur. and Wit. John Mountague and Thomas Hill. p.10.

VAUGHAN, Dudley and Judith Garton, widow. Bond 19 December 1801. Sur.
and Wit. David Garland. p.53.

VOWELL, David and Mary Bird. Bond 15 June 1796. Sur. and Wit. James
Mickelburrough and Anney Farr. p.45.

WAGNER, David Van and Emily F. Crittenden. Bond 24 January 1850. Married __ January 1850 by Thomas B. Evans. Emily's father gives
consent in person. [name not given.] Sur. and Wit. James D.
Crittenden. p.138.

WAKE, Ambrose and Miss Anna H. Boss. Bond 5 July 1814. Sur. and Wit.
James Burke and Jeremiah Jackson. p.77.

WAKE, Christopher and Sarah Sommers. Bond 26 December 1789. Married
28 December 1789 by Samuel Klug. Sur. and Wit. Francis Ross. p.35.

WAKE, Johnston and Nancy Jackson. Bond 30 December 1780. Sur. and Wit. William Jackson. p.24.

WAKE, Leroy and Betsey G. Garland. Bond 1 August 1821. John B. Garland, father of Betsey. Sur. and Wit. John B. Garland. p.85.

WAKE, Leroy D., Jr. and Martha A. Pitts. Consent dated 27 September 1852. Sur. and Wit. John J. Wake. [Consent only.] p.143.

WAKE, Ransone and Mary Elliott, of lawful age. Bond 7 February 1803. Sur. and Wit. William Wake. p. 56.

WAKE, Robert and Ann Elliott. Bond 31 January 1788. Married 1 February 1788 by Samuel Klug. Sur. and Wit. Jeremiah Powell. p.32.

WAKE, Robert and Ester Standard. Bond 7 January 1808. Married 7 January 1808 by David Corey. Sur. and Wit. James Stiff and John B. Long. p.66.

WAKE, Thomas N. and Miss Margaret T. Carter, of lawful age. Bond 17 May 1819. Sur. and Wit. Thomas Edwards. p.84.

WAKE, William and Lucy Billups Powell, age 21. Bond 17 December 1799. Married 21 December 1799 by Henry Heffernan. Jeremiah and Agnes Powell, parents of Lucy who was born August 1778. Sur. and Wit. James Ross, Elizabeth Garland, and Staige Davis. p.50.

WALDEN, Edward and Miss Mary M. H. Watts. Bond 7 November 1827. Ralph Watt, father of Mary. Sur. and Wit. John Walden. p.98.

WALDEN, Edward and Rebecca Owen. Bond 1 April 1839. Sur. and Wit. Elliott Gardner and Larkin Gardner. p.118.

WALDEN, Edwin and Rebecca Owen. Bond 1 April 1839. Sur. and Wit. Elliot Gardner and Larkin Gardner. p. 119. [Apparently same as above.]

WALDEN, Enos and Miss Elizabeth Newcomb. Bond 11 October 1845. Sur. and Wit. John Walden. p.129.

WALDEN, John and Miss Maria Kidd. Bond 26 September 1822. Henry Kidd, deceased, father of Maria. Sur. and Wit. Lewis Walden. p.86.

WALDEN, John, of Mathews County, and Miss Eleanor Hodgers, 21 years of age. Bond 3 February 1832. Sur. and Wit. Lewis Shackelford. p.107.

WALDEN, John and Miss Sarah Gardner. Bond 5 March 1845. Married __ March 1845 by Thomas B. Evans. Sur. and Wit. Henry Sears. p.127.

WALDEN, Lewis and Judith Kidd. Bond 28 July 1788. Married 6 September 1788 by Samuel Klug. Sur. and Wit. Henry Kidd and Isaac Carleton. p. 32.

WALDEN, Lewis, Jr., and Miss Lydia Watts. Bond 9 October 1815.
  Ralph Watts, father of Lydia. Sur. and Wit. Joseph Hardy. p.79.

WALDEN, Robert and Miss Frances D. Sibley. Bond 26 February 1827.
  Married 26 February 1827 by Richard Claybrook. [Repeated in
  marriage register with date of 1 March 1827.] Sur. and Wit.
  Edmond Healy. p.96.

WALDEN, William and Elizabeth S. Daniel. Bond 16 May 1851. Married
  __ May 1851 by Thomas B. Evans. Sur. and Wit. John C. Daniel. p.140.

WALKER, Cornelius and Miss Emaline Palmer. Bond 22 June 1846. Married
  23 June 1846 by George Northam. Sur. and Wit. Robert Blake and
  M. J. M. Walker. p. 131.

WALKER, Edwin C. and Mary A. Clare. Married 16 May 1852 by R. A.
  Christian. [Minister's return only.] p.169.

WALKER, Francis, widower and Miss Hannah Reveer. Bond 7 June 1814.
  Sur. and Wit. George Reveer and Peter Reveer. p.77.

WALKER, Francis M. and Elizabeth Ann Creighton. Bond 9 April 1850.
  Married 11 April 1850 by Holland Walker. J. A. Creighton, father
  of Elizabeth. Sur. and Wit. W. T. Miles. p.138.

WALKER, George and Miss Julia Joanna Blake. Bond 29 August 1820.
  Robert N. Blake, father of Julia. Sur. and Wit. Moses Walker, Jr.
  p.85.

WALKER, Hiram and Miss Eliza L. Barrick. Bond 28 March 1826. Robert
  Barrick, father of Eliza. Sur. and Wit. William S. Robinson. p.94.

WALKER, Holland and Ann M. Reveer. Bond 22 May 1837. Married 25 May
  1837 by George Northam. Sur. and Wit. Hiram Walker. p.117.

WALKER, Holland and Julia J. Walker. Bond 28 March 1848. Married
  29 March 1848 by R. A. Christian. Sur. and Wit. Robert Blake and
  Alice F. Robinson. p.133.

WALKER, Joel and Miss Polley C. Robinson. Bond 19 December 1832.
  Peter Robinson, father of Polley. Sur. and Wit. Robert Blake. p.110.

WALKER, Moses, Jr. and Miss Mary J. Humphries, both of lawful age.
  Bond 9 January 1821. Sur. and Wit. Nelson Humphries. p.85.

WALKER, Moses J. M. and Sarah F. Reveer. Bond 25 March 1844. Married
  26 March 1844 by George Northam. Sur. and Wit. George B. Reveer
  and Cornelius Walker. p.125.

WALLER, John and Nancy Sears. Married 7 March 1799 by Henry Heffernan.
  [Minister's return only.] p.153.

WARE, Arthur and Mary Bryant. Bond 28 March 1774. Sur. and Wit. James Ware and Jasper Clayton. p.20.

WARE, James and Jean McKan. Bond 20 July 1773. Sur. and Wit. James Mackan and Wm Blackburn. p.18.

WARE, John and Miss Francis McKan. Bond 8 November 1815. Leonard Jackson, guardian of Francis. Sur. and Wit. John Daniel. p.79.

WARE, John and Miss Elizabeth Jones. Bond 19 December 1832. Richard Jones, father of Elizabeth. Sur. and Wit. Richard H. Street and F. Blackburn. p.110.

WARE, Reubin and Miss Sarah Hardy. Bond 20 December 1826. Joseph Hardy, father of Sarah. Sur. and Wit. Thomas Hall. p.95.

WARE, Robert and Catharine McKan. Bond 20 July 1773. Sur. and Wit. James Mackan and William Blackburn. p.18.

WARE, Robert and Penny Daniel. Bond 20 October 1794. Sur. and Wit. William Brooking, Phillip Lee, and Ann Lee. p.42.

WARE, Robert and Miss Catharine Dillard. Bond 31 October 1846. Catharine Dillard, mother of Catharine. Sur. and Wit. William H. Haile and Thomas Montague. p.131.

WARE, Robert E. and Miss Charlotte Lee, age of 21 years. Bond 28 May 1810. Sur. and Wit. Charles Lee. p.70.

WARE, Samuel and Nancy Shipley, in 25th year. Bond 14 June 1799. Nathan Shipley, father of Nancy. Sur. and Wit. Robert Shepherd, Lydia Daniel, and Elizabeth H. Daniel. p.50.

WARING, Henry and Lucia Stiff. Bond 6 April 1830. Married 7 April 1830 by George Northam. C. Braxton, guardian of Lucia. Sur. and Wit. Thomas Street. p.103.

WARWICK, John C., over 21 years of age, and Mary Wake, over 21 years of age. Bond 29 November 1800. Sur. and Wit. Robert Wake. p.51.

WASHINGTON, Henry and Miss Anne Thacker. Bond 9 January 1749. Sur. and Wit. Henry Willis. p.5.

WASHINGTON, Henry and Charlotte Mountague, widow. Bond 3 March 1760. Sur. and Wit. Lewis Mountague. p.11.

WATSON, Robert and Mary Hibble. Bond 29 July 1793. Sur. and Wit. Braxton Dunlevy. p.40.

WATSON, William and Parmelia Young. Bond 24 May 1848. Married 30 May 1848 by Holland Walker. [In the marriage register the word Negroes is written in a different handwriting from that of the copyist. Nowhere on the bond is it so stated.] Sur. and Wit. Robert N. Trice. p.134.

WATTS, Charles and Maria Dunn. Bond 26 November 1810. Agrippa Dunn, father of Maria. Sur. and Wit. Dabney A. Miller and John Purks. p.71.

WATTS, Charles and Miss Rebecca Ware, of age. Bond 2 November 1812. Sur. and Wit. Major Wyatt. p.75.

WATTS, Charles and Miss Frances Watts. Bond 7 November 1827. Sur. and Wit. Thomas Hundley, Jr. p.98.

WATTS, George S. and Mary E. O'Neal. Bond 27 March 1848. "Issued by the personal consent of the guardian." [No name.] Sur. and Wit. James L. Noel. p.133.

WATTS, James and Miss Frances Purks. Bond 7 April 1828. John Purks, deceased, father of Frances and Lewis B. Montague, guardian. Sur. and Wit. James Gardner and John Watts. p.97.

WATTS, Ralph and Polly Williams. Bond 27 June 1796. Sur. and Wit. James Stamper. p.45.

WATTS, William and Elizabeth Thurston. Bond 16 November 1815. Elizabeth is widow of William D. Thurston, deceased, and signs her own consent. Sur. and Wit. Allen Howard. p.79.

WEBB, William Crittenden and Fanny Wortham. Bond 9 July 1789. Married 11 July 1789 by Samuel Klug. Sur. and Wit. Thomas Churchhill. p.34.

WEBMORE, John and Frances Jones. Bond 15 December 1785. Married 18 December 1785 by Samuel Klug. Sur. and Wit. Edmond Webmore. p.29.

WEDMORE, John and Miss Ann Robinson. Bond 27 January 1812. Sur. and Wit. William Robinson and John Robinson. p.73.

WEDMORE (WEBMORE), William J. and Elizabeth Robinson. Bond 20 February 1816. William Robinson, deceased, father of Elizabeth, who signs her own consent. Sur. and Wit. William Robinson and John Robinson. p.80.

WELLFORD, Charles C. and Miss Mary C. Stiff. Bond 17 March 1824. Married 18 March 1824 by Ira Parker. Thomas Stiff, deceased, father of Mary. Sur. and Wit. John A. G. Davis. p.89.

WEST, George and Winney Shelton. Bond 23 August 1779. Sur. and Wit. William Robinson. p.23.

WEST, George and Frances Barrick. Bond 18 July 1788. Married 20 July 1788 by Samuel Klug. Sur. and Wit. Daniel Jefferson. p.32.

WHEELER, Carter and Miss Virginia Brooke, under 21. Bond 24 August 1835. Taver Brook, mother of Virginia. Sur. and Wit. David Bunting, Richard C. Muse, and James H. Thurston. p.116.

WHITE, Thomas and Julia Wilkins. Married 25 September 1837 by George Northam. [Minister's return only.] p.161.

WHITELEY, John and Priscilla Chowning. Bond 31 May 1794. Sur. and Wit. Charles Whitaker. p.42.

WHITELY, John and Sally Sanders. Bond 25 December 1787. Married 25 December 1787 by Samuel Klug. Sur. and Wit. Benjamin Deagle and Thomas Churchhill. p.32.

WHITING, Matthew, Jr. and Elizabeth Robinson, spinster. Bond 31 March 1763. Sur. and Wit. John Robinson. p.14.

WIATT, James and Fanny Curtis. Bond 8 October 1798. Married 10 October 1798 by Henry Heffernan. Sur. and Wit. Cary Kemp. p.48.

WIATT, Elijah and Nancy Wiatt. Married 15 November 1810 by Philip Montague. [Minister's return only.] p.156.

WIATT, Henry T. and Martha Simco. Married 1 July 1825 by Richard Claybrook. [Minister's return only.] p.157.

WILKINS, James and Elizabeth Snelling. Bond 6 January 1786. Sur. and Wit. Daniel Jefferson. p.29.

WILKINS, John and Lucy Gibson. Bond 25 August 1788. Married 31 August 1788 by Samuel Klug. Sur. and Wit. John Berry. p.33.

WILKINS, John and Miss Ann Parrott, who signs own consent. Bond 13 May 1816. Sur. and Wit. George W. Layton, Nelson Humphries, Jr., and Nancy Parrott. p.81.

WILKINS, Robert, of age, and Avery Fenning. Bond 27 October 1810. James Parker, stepfather of Avery, gives affidavit that she is "more than 21 years." Sur. and Wit. James Parker. p.71.

WILLIAMS, Austin and Miss Juliet Spann, of lawful age. Bond 19 June 1829. Married 26 June 1829 by George Northam. Sur. and Wit. Robert Dunlavey. p. 102.

WILLIAMS, Benjamin and Esther Smith. Bond 23 February 1778. Sur. and Wit. John George. p.22.

WILLIAMS, Carter and Ann Stamper, who signs her own consent. Bond 2 August 1815. John Stamper, deceased, father of Ann. Sur. and Wit. Samuel Stamper. p.79.

WILLIAMS, Carter and Frances Gibson. Bond 3 January 1843. Married 3 January 1843 by Richard A. Christian. Sur. and Wit. William H. Newcomb, Louisa Newcomb, and Nancey Williams. p.122.

WILLIAMS, Christopher S. and Miss Annah Gardner. Bond 26 December 1843. Sur. and Wit. James H. Hackney, John J. Muse, and Curtis Williams. p.124.

WILLIAMS, George and Hannah Watts, of age. Bond 26 October 1793. Married 31 October 1793 by John Mullins. Sarah Watts, mother of Hannah. Sur. and Wit. Robert Watson and P. Blackburn. p. 41.

WILLIAMS, George and Catharine Bennett, of lawful age. Bond 27 June 1803. Thomas Bennett, Sr., father of Catharine. Sur. and Wit. John Thruston. p.56.

WILLIAMS, George B. and Mrs. Elizabeth F. Coats. Bond 3 May 1848. Married 4 May 1848 by R. A. Christian. Elizabeth is relict of William Coats, deceased. Sur. and Wit. Thomas B. South and William C. Edwards. p.134.

WILLIAMS, James and Miss Mary Thruston (Thurston) who signs own consent. Bond 5 June 1817. William Thurston, deceased, father of Mary. Sur. and Wit. Carter Williams. p.83.

WILLIAMS, John F. and Miss Ann C. Parron. Bond 12 August 1845. Sur. and Wit. Lewis Williams, Lewis B. Montague, and William Parron. p.129.

WILLIAMS, Lewis and Sally Williamson, widow. Bond 25 February 1799. Sur. and Wit. Bivvin Abbott and Peter Kemp, Jr. p.49.

WILLIAMS, Lewis and Miss Lany Christopher. Bond 25 December 1826. Sur. and Wit. George Northam and George S. Pace. p.96.

WILLIAMS, Lewis and Miss Sarah E. McTyre. Bond 18 September 1843. Sur. and Wit. George W. Sadler, John A. Montague, and Zach Street. p.123.

WILLIAMS, William, over 21 years, and Ann Boss, over 21 years. Bond 2 February 1806. Married 7 February 1807 by David Corey. Lewis Boss, father of Ann. Sur. and Wit. William Hammond. p.61.

WILLIAMSON, Benjamin H. and Sarah Chowning. Bond 18 December 1811. Robert Chowning, deceased, father of Sarah, John Saunders, guardian. Sur. and Wit. John Saunders. p.73.

WILLIAMSON, Isham and Nancy Parron. Bond 25 April 1791. Married 30 April 1791 by John Mullins. Sur. and Wit. William Shackelford and Robert Stamper. p.36.

WILLIAMSON, Nelson and Sally Weatherspon. Bond 19 December 1785. Married 25 December 1785 by Samuel Klug. Benjamin Williamson, father of Nelson. Elizabeth Weatherspon, mother of Sally. Sur. and Wit. William Kidd. p.29.

WILLS, Thomas and Sarah Dean. Bond 24 September 1773. Sur. and Wit. David Dickinson and Will Dawson. p. 18.

WILSON, David M. and Elizabeth Christopher, over 21 years. Bond 5 August 1837. Married 15 November 1837 by George Northam. p.117.

WILSON, Lafayette and Mary C. Montgomery. Bond 1 July 1847. Sur. and Wit. James H. Prichett and James Montgomery. p.132.

WILSON, Robert and Betty Payne. Bond 23 September 1786. Sur. and Wit. William Wilson. p.30.

WILSON, Robert and Rutha Meigs. Bond 2 April 1817. James Meigs, father of Rutha. Sur. and Wit. Robert Meigs. p.82.

WILTSHIRE, Benjamin and Nancy Kidd. Bond 5 September 1806. Married 5 September 1806 by Henry Heffernan. Nancy is widow of Robert Kidd, deceased. Sur. and Wit. Griffin McTuggle and Bivvin Abbott. p.62.

WINNING, Niels and Ann Humphris. Bond 17 December 1787. Married 24 December 1787 by Samuel Klug. Sur. and Wit. William Jones. p.31.

WOOD, Curtis and Miss Elizabeth Brim. Bond 20 February 1817. Samuel Wood gives consent for his son. Leonard Brim, father of Elizabeth. Sur. and Wit. Leonard Brim, Charles Lee, Henry A. Howard, and Mrs. Elizabeth Brim. p.82.

WOOD, Curtis and Miss Sarah Haile. Bond 29 December 1834. Sur. and Wit. John Brim and Robert McKan. p.115.

WOOD, James U. and Miss Mary M. Mountain. Bond 19 November 1822. John B. Mountain, deceased, father of Mary, and Carter Purkins, guardian. Sur. and Wit. Robert Mountain. p.86.

WOOD, John and Nancy Longest. Bond 31 March 1788. Married 2 April 1788 by Samuel Klug. Sur. and Wit. Nicholas Wood. p.32.

WOOD, John and Miss Mary J. Berry. Bond 15 February 1810. Thomas Healy, Jr., guardian of Mary. Sur. and Wit. Samuel B. Wood and Houlder H. Berry. p.69.

WOOD, John and Miss Elizabeth Faucett. Bond 12 August 1812. Vincent W. Faucett, guardian of Elizabeth. Sur. and Wit. Vincent W. Faucett. p.75.

WOOD, Lewis Lee and Miss Mary Ann Bristow. Bond 6 February 1834. Married 6 February 1834 by Richard Claybrook. William Bristow, deceased, father, and Agnes Bristow, mother of Mary Ann. Sur. and Wit. Robert Bray and Robert H. Dunlevy. p.113.

WOOD, Samuel and Sarah Watts. Bond 23 January 1796. Sur. and Wit. Newbill Dunn and Christopher Robinson. p.44.

WOOD, Samuel and Mrs. Judith B. Daniel, who signs own consent. Bond
16 January 1817. Judith is widow of Beverly Daniel, deceased. Sur.
and Wit. Dabney A. Miller and Phil. T. Montague. p.82.

WOOD, Samuel and Miss Julia Watts. Bond 12 March 1822. Ralph Watts,
father of Julia. Sur. and Wit. Philip Montague, Jr. p.87.

WOOD, Samuel and Catharine Gardner. Bond 23 January 1832. Larkin
Gardner swears Catharine is of the age of 21. Sur. and Wit. Larkin
Gardner. p.107.

WOOD, Samuel Blake and Polly Clarke Healy. Bond 16 December 1803.
William Wood, father of Samuel. Captain James Healy, father of
Polly. Sur. and Wit. James Healy, Samuel Blake, and Elizabeth W.
Wood. p.57.

WOOD, THOLOMEAH (Tholly M.) and Betsy Upshaw Garland. Bond 24 February
1798. David Garland gives consent for Betsy. Sur. and Wit. George
Blackley. p.48.

WOOD, Thomas and Miss Sally Watts. Bond 21 December 1824. Sur. and
Wit. Charles Watts. p.90.

WOOD, William and Fanny Blake. Bond 3 December 1774. Sur. and Wit.
Jacob Blake. p.20.

WOOD, William, Jr. and Fanny Jones. Bond 7 February 1791. Sur. and
Wit. Gabriel Jones. p.36.

WOOD, William B. and Miss Ann Jackson. Bond 3 January 1834. John S.
Boss, guardian of Ann. Sur. and Wit. William S. Berry. p. 113.

WOOD, William H. and Miss Eliza Bray. Bond 14 December 1830. Sur.
and Wit. Robert Bray. p.104.

WOODDY, Robert and Polly Corey. Bond 23 August 1813. John Wooddy, Sr.,
guardian of Robert. David Corey, deceased, father of Polly. Sur.
and Wit. Thomas Healy and John Wooddy, Jr. p.76.

WOODLEY, John and Mary Jefferson. Bond 16 January 1789. Married
19 January 1789 by Samuel Klug. Daniel Jefferson, father of Mary.
Sur. and Wit. William Jones and Thomas Kemp. p.34.

WOODLEY, John and Betsy Hunt, 21 years and upwards. Bond 22 February
1806. Married 22 February 1806 by William Frichett of Mathews
County. Sur. and Wit. James Parker and Nelson Humphries. p.61.

WOODLEY, Thomas and Mary Minter. Bond 23 December 1796. Married
25 December 1796 by Henry Heffernan. Sur. and Wit. John Minter.
p.46.

WOODS, John and Elizabeth Brooks. Bond 15 December 1785. Married
17 December 1785 by Samuel Klug. Sur. and Wit. William Jones. p.29.

WOODS, John and Miss Elizabeth Davis, 21 years of age. Bond 18 October 1814. James Davis, deceased, father of Elizabeth. Sur. and Wit. William Hill. p.78.

WOODS, Thomas and Ellen Davis, both of age 21. Bond 29 September 1810. James Davis, Sr., deceased, father of Ellen. Sur. and Wit. William Hill. p.71.

WOODS, Thomas and Mrs. Avery Wilkins. Bond 29 January 1817. Avery is widow of Robert Wilkins, deceased, and signs own consent. Sur. and Wit. Nelson Humphries, Jr. p.82.

WOODS, Thomas and Mehala Boss. Bond 12 March 1824. Mehala is widow of John Boss. Sur. and Wit. John Woods. p.89.

WOODWARD, Thomas H. and Lucy Elizabeth B. Roane. Bond 12 November 1839. Married 14 November 1839 by George Northam. Sur. and Wit. James A. Eubank and John S. Healy. p.119.

WORTHAM, Coleman and Eunice B. Shepherd. Bond 14 June 1849. Married 14 June 1849 by R. A. Christian. "Issued by the personal consent of guardian." [No name shown.] Sur. and Wit. Richard W. Scott. p.134.

WORTHAM, George and Sarah C. Palmer, age of 21 years. Bond 25 October 1815. David Palmer, father of Sarah. Sur. and Wit. Thomas Palmer. p.79.

WORTHAM, James and Frankey Smith. Bond 3 January 1778. Sur. and Wit. Samuel Klug. p.22.

WORTHAM, John and Catharine George. Bond 8 February 1790. Married 14 February 1790 by Samuel Klug. Sur. and Wit. Benjamin Hackney and Thomas Iverson. p.35.

WORTHAM, Meacham and Joanna Wake. Bond 7 November 1795. Married 14 November 1795 by Henry Heffernan. Sur. and Wit. Henry Kidd. p.44.

WORTHAM, Meacham and Lucy Bristow. Married 6 January 1802 by Henry Heffernan. [Minister's return only.] p.154.

WORTHAM, Samuel and Ann Wortham. Bond 14 July 1763. George Wortham, deceased, father of Ann; Thomas Laughlin gives consent. Sur. and Wit. James Wortham, William Bickham, and Elizabeth Elliot. p.14.

WORTHAM, William and Miss Anna Frances Montague. Bond 13 May 1823. Sur. and Wit. Augustine Owen, Philip Montague, and Labon Corr. p.87.

WRIGHT, Thomas, Jr. and Miss Mary Elizabeth Shepherd. Bond 21 September 1825. Married 22 September 1825 by Richard Claybrook. Sur. and Wit. William Jesse and Lucy Shepherd. p.92.

WRIGHT, John R. and Miss Elizabeth R. B. Woodward. Bond 10 January
1843. Married 12 January 1843 by Thomas B. Evans. Mrs. Elizabeth
R. Woodward, mother of Elizabeth. Sur. and Wit. Thomas B. Evans.
p.122

WRIGHT, Wiley and Miss Mary E. Shepherd. Bond 23 March 1844. Married
__ March 1844 by Thomas B. Evans. Thomas Street, guardian of Mary.
Sur. and Wit. Thomas Street. p.125.

WYATT, Elijah and Nancy Wyatt. Bond 27 October 1810. Henry Wyatt,
deceased, father of Nancy. Sur. and Wit. Joseph Godwin and Caty
Wyatt. p.71.

WYATT, Henry and Caty Turner. Bond 28 November 1785. Married 23 December 1785 by Samuel Klug. Sur. and Wit. Wyatt Gibson. p.29.

WYATT, Henry T. and Martha Simco (Sinco), 21 years of age. Bond
1 July 1825. Sur. and Wit. Elijah Wyatt and George Heart. p.92.

WYATT, Joseph and Elizabeth Turner. Bond 22 January 1783. Thomas
Turner, father of Elizabeth. Sur. and Wit. William Wyatt, Major
Wyatt, and Thomas Turner, Jr. p.26.

WYATT, Major and Susanna Ware, of age. Bond 10 June 1812. Sur. and
Wit. Robert Palmer, Selly Daniel, and Elebeth Wyatt. p.74.

WYATT, Richard H. and Frances Walden. Bond 16 December 1839. Sur.
and Wit. Henry Sears. p.119.

WYATT, Thomas and Miss Margaret Brooking. Bond 11 March 1833. Sur.
and Wit. Lawrence Crouch. p.111.

WYATT, Thomas and Nancy Sears. Bond 16 August 1848. Sur. and Wit.
Elliott Gardner and Robert M. Haile. p.134.

YARRINGTON, John and Miss Mary Bryant. Bond 23 July 1752. Sur. and
Wit. Benjamin Rhodes. p.6.

YARRINGTON, Oliver and Elizabeth Ware. Bond 12 July 1785. Married
15 July 1785 by Samuel Klug. Sur. and Wit. Philip Sears. p.28.

YARRINGTON, Philip and Judith Jones. Bond 7 September 1787. Married
8 September 1787 by Samuel Klug. William Jones, father of Judith.
Sur. and Wit. Thomas Clare and P. Blackburn. p.31.

YARRINGTON, Vincent and Elizabeth B. Stiff. Bond 4 November 1795.
Married 5 November 1795 by Henry Heffernan. William Stiff, grandfather of Elizabeth, gives consent. Sur. and Wit. Sarah Churchill.
p.43.

YATES, Bartholomew and Elizabeth Stanard. Bond 9 September 1741. Sur. and Wit. John Reade and Christopher Curtis. p. 1.

YATES, Harry Beverley and Lucy Murray. Bond 19 May 1779. Rachel Murray, mother of Lucy. Sur. and Wit. Samuel Klug and William Murray. p.22.

YATES, Harry Beverley and Jane Montague. Bond 24 February 1783. Sur. and Wit. Thomas Segar. p.27.

YOUNG, William and Jane Mickelburrough. Bond 7 April 1773. Henry Mickelburrough, Sr., father of Jane. Sur. and Wit. James Mickelburrough and Mary Mickelburrough. p.17.

FEMALE INDEX

A

Abbott,
Elizabeth	35
Fanny	17
Jane	50

Adkins,
Catherine	76

Adkinson,
Catharine	48,76

Ailworth, Ailsworth
Eliza A.	38
Eliza Ann	40
Maria	52
Milkey	27

Alderson,
Nancy	22

Aldin, Alldin
Elizabeth	33
Frances	27
Jane	54

Allen,
Caty	54
Elizabeth	78
Margaret	17

Alliot,
Mary	1

Anderson,
Mary	22

Anderton,
Elizabeth	17,40
Mary Frances	38
Sarah E.	1

Armistead,
Harriet	76

Ashton,
Anna Maria	27

Atkins,
Mary	49

Atkinson,
Eliza	18
Mary	10

B

Badley,
Elizabeth P.	72

Baker,
Elizabeth	7
Mary Ann	77
Sarah	63

Barnes,
Betsa	73

Barnrick,
Martha	18

Barrick, Barrock
Amanda	66
Ann	76
Catharine E.	80
Diana	42
Eliza	5
Eliza L.	88
Elizabeth	9,80
Elizabeth J.	64
Frances	90
Louisa	63
Louisa C.	86
Lucy	61
Mary Ann	58
Mary Ann S.	61
Nancy	47
Priscilla	44
Sarah	32,68
Sarah S.	77

Batchelder, Batcheldor
Ann	34,59
Anne Anderson	2
Catherine	80
Elizabeth	66,86
Frances	6,54,79
Jane	63
Molly	27
Sarah	56
Susannah B.	68

(1)

Bawl,		
Frances A.	65	
Bayley,		
Elizabeth	27	
Bayton,		
Sarah	10	
Beaman, Beamon		
Ann	29	
Jane	76	
Beazeley, Beazley		
Jane E. P.	21	
Martha Ann	82	
Melvina L.	77	
Beddoo,		
Bethuel	63	
Elizabeth Frances	11	
Bennett,		
Catharine	58,92	
Elizabeth B.	81	
Mary	14	
Mary Ann	4	
Nancy	36	
Winney	63	
Berkeley,		
Elizabeth B.	18	
Lucy Nelson	40	
Mary	19	
Berry,		
Ann	9	
Frances	85	
Henritta	21	
Maria	20	
Martha Ann	52	
Mary	28	
Mary Ann	22	
Mary J.	93	
Polly H.	15	
Susan J.	52	
Billups,		
Lucy	38	
Bird,		
Frances	29	
Lavinia	4	
Mary	86	

Blackburn,		
Elizabeth	41	
Hannah	45	
Jean	24	
Mary	71	
Melicent	45	
Virginia S.	26	
Blackley,		
Elizabeth	72	
Francis	41	
Jane W.	85	
Blade, Blaid		
Elizabeth	46	
Mary	15	
Nancy	51	
Permilia	22	
Blake,		
Alice	25,70	
Ann	27,28,42	
Betty	80	
Cordelia	8	
Eleanor	84	
Eliza N.	27	
Elizabeth	13	
Elizabeth Robinson	7	
Fanny	94	
Frances	41,68	
Johanna	51	
Julia Joanna	88	
Juliann	76	
Letitia A.	68	
Lucy	7,23	
Mary	72	
Mary L.	8	
Nancy	3	
Polly Long	31	
Sarah	8,40,43,51	
Susan	6	
Susanna	15,70	
Blakey,		
Adeline F.	53	
Ann	48	
Catharine	17	
Elizabeth	52,82	
Maria Ann Catharine	56	
Sarah E. R.	63	
Bland,		
Emily	72	
Julia Ann E.	78	
Louisa	45	
Mary Susan	69	

Blueford,
    Elizabeth   20

Boldry,
    Letitia   8

Boss,
    Ann   92
    Anna H.   43,86
    Caty   22
    Eliza Ann   13
    Martha   59
    Mehala   95
    Susannah   11,25

Boughton,
    Susanna   20

Bowcock,
    Elizabeth   15

Bower,
    Ann   62

Bray,
    Ann H.   39
    Dorothy   29
    Eliza   94
    Frances   15
    Johnna   2
    Lucy Ann   12
    Mary   67
    Susanna   2

Brim,
    Elizabeth   93
    Jane   16

Bristow,
    Elizabeth   10,11,40
    Elizabeth D.   2
    Eudora   13
    Fanny   12
    Frances C.   33
    Lucy   29,95
    Lucy Ann   35
    Lucy B.   52
    Maria D.   55
    Mary   54
    Mary Ann   39,93
    Mary Frances   32
    Polly   11
    Rebecca   70
    Sarah   47
    Sarah C.   16
    Sarah E.   10   (3)

Brooke,
    Frances   18
    Virginia   90

Brooking
    Addy (Addeline)   23
    Margaret   96

Brooks,
    Elizabeth   71,94
    Frances   12
    Lucy E.   20
    Sarah   41

Brown,
    Catharine   16
    Frances S.   33
    Mary   58
    Mildred   42
    Nancy   11

Brummell,
    Mary   7

Bryant,
    Betty   51
    Mary   89,96

Burk,
    Eliza[a]   85

Burns,
    Mary   14

Burton,
    Ann   2,20
    Elizabeth   44,49
    Mary   53
    Milley   65

Burwell,
    Sarah Nelson   61

C

Callehan,
    Ann   15

Campbell,
    Fanny   43
    Martha   27

Carter,
    Margaret T.   87
    Mary   37

Carter (continued)
Mary Almedia 38
Pelina J. 37

Carwick,
Catherine 5

Cauthorne,
Eglantine E. 60

Chapman,
Jane 40
Lucy Ann 52

Cheney,
Catherine 14

Chowning,
Ann 8
Catharine 17
Eunice B. 75
Frances 45
Lucy 81
Mary Jane 39
Matilda B. 64
Nancy 31
Priscilla 91
Rachel 48
Sarah 92

Christian
Elizabeth G. 42
Hester 56
Mary S 31
Tabitha 17

Christopher,
Elizabeth 93
Hester Ann 58
Lany 92
Mary 67
Nancy 58

Churchhill, Churchill
Betty 46
Betty Carter 31
Hannah 69
Lucy 35
Mrs. Lucy B. 24
Lucy Harrison 24
Mary 2
Priscilla 79

Clare,
Lucinda B. 31
Lucy 23
Mary A. 88
Martha 37
Martha Ann 68
Rosy 59

Clark, Clarke,
Elizabeth 83
Mrs. Elizabeth 76
Frances 81
Lillian H. 65
Louisa 76
Martha J. 45
Mary 60
Polly 81
Sarah 26

Claudas, Claudus, Cloudis,
Betsey 66
Frances 62
Lucy 68
Nancy 19
Penelope 51

Claybrook,
A. H. 79
Amanda 57
Fanny B. 30
Mary D. 45

Clayton,
Julia Ann 42
Verlinda L. 69

Clayville,
Comfort 25

Clear,
Mrs. Frances 75

Cloughton,
Nancy 69

Coats,
Mrs. Elizabeth F. 92

Collier,
Catey 73
Susanna 31

Cooke,
Crissy 5

Cooke (continued)

Lucy E.	30
Molly	79

Cooper,

Nancy	22

Corbin,

Betty Tayloe	21,60,86
Edmonia Fauntleroy	16
Juliet T.	40

Corey,

Harriott	58
Polly	94

Cornelius,

Catharine	65
Hannah	38
Jane	86

Corr,

Frances E.	28,73

Craine,

Eleanor	38

Creighton,

Elizabeth Ann	88
Lauretta (Loretta)	55

Crittenden,

Catharine C.	37
Emily F.	86
Polly	69

Crossfield,

Catharine	37
Nancy	12
Sally	84

Crosswell,

Maria Jane	19

Cundiff, Cundieff

Mrs. Catherine	31
Elizabeth Jane	20
Mary Ann	18,62
Nancy K.	84

Curtis,

Fanny	91
Polly Murray	2

D

Dallam,

Betty T. C.	39

Dame,

Mary	44

Daniel,

Anne C.	19
Betty L.	13
Clara	8
Constant	84
Eleanor C.	53
Eliza T.	74
Elizabeth	26,41,49
Elizabeth A.	42
Elizabeth S.	88
Esther	75
Frances	19,23
Jenny	53
Judith	75
Mrs. Judith B.	94
Judith E.	14
Louisa M.	51
Lucy	46
Mrs. Lucy	24
Lucy Ann	24
Lydia	23
Maria Adeline	9
Mary	23,37,75
Mary E.	65
Mary F.	81
Nancy	53
Peggy	83
Penny	89
Rachel	60
Sally	84,86
Sally R.	62
Sarah	19,47,69
Susanna	54
Susanna George	33

Davis,

Alice	26
Ann	68
Catharine	43
Eliza	48
Elizabeth	6,42,81,95
Ellen	95
Jenetta	32
Louisa A.	53
Louisa E.	50
Lucy	5,25

Davis (continued)

Maria G.	10
Martha	59
Mary	49,51
Mary F.	64
Matilda	60
Nancy	41
Sarah	58
Susannah	41

Deagle, Degle

Ann	65
Elizabeth	65
Martha Ann	5
Mary Jane	23
Nancy J.	34
Patsey	85
Rebecca	29

Dean,

Elizabeth	55
Sarah	93

Deaton,

Caroline	66

Dejarnett

Nancy	1

Dickie,

Anna D.	52

Didlake,

Catharine B.	20
Jane	4
Martha M.	74
Polly D.	34

Dillard

Catharine	89
Elizabeth	4
Nancy	48
Patsey	85
Sarah Major	21

Dobson,

Susan	75

Dudley,

Ann	23,43
Elizabeth	82
Jane	5,10,18,52,74,82
Mrs. Lucy	35
Mary	79
Mary Ann	32

Dudley (continued)

Mildred	1
Mrs. Priscilla	60
Rebecca	43

Duncan,

Emeline	3
Kesiah A.	7

Dungee,

Sarah	28

Dunlavey,

Elizabeth	72
Nancy	56
Rebecca	67

Dunlavy,

Amanda	31
Nancy	44
Sarah	78
Sarah E.	61

Dunlevy,

Ann	70
Elizabeth H.	37
Lucy	31

Dunn,

Alcia (Alice)	66
Catharine	56
Mrs. Elizabeth	35
Frances	42
Lucy	58
Nancy	75,80
Maria	90
Polly	84
Sarah	75

E

Edwards,

Malissa C.	78
Miry Ann	72

Elgar,

Jenetta	40
Narcissa	50

Elliott,

Ann	87
Dorothy	83
Mary	66,87

Evans,

Adeline	9

Fagan,
  Martha   3

Farrow,
  Anna   20

Faucett,
  Elizabeth   93

Faulkner,
  Judith   9
  Nancy   6
  Sarah   72

Fauntleroy,
  Catherine   21

Fearn,
  Ann   69
  Dorothy   69
  Judith   30
  Mary   63

Fenning,
  Avery   91
  Mary   65

Fisher,
  Polly   41

Fitzgerald
  Henrietta   25
  Priscilla   85

Fitzhugh,
  Elizabeth Henry   22

Fogg,
  Mary F.   39

Forest,
  Mary   62

Foster,
  Maria E.D.   73

French,
  Elizabeth   11
  Frances   47
  Mary   40

Gaines,
  Mary   82

Games,
  Ann C. D.   17

Gardner,
  Ann C.   32
  Annah   92
  Catharine   94
  Frances   47
  Sarah   87

Garland,
  Betsey G.   87
  Betsy Upshaw   94
  Dalinda   78
  Elizabeth   34
  Mary   15,62,71

Garrett,
  Agnes   13
  Elizabeth   23
  Frances   33,52
  Margaret M.   21
  Martha A.   2
  Mary   13
  Mary E.   50
  Nancy   35
  Olivia A.   65
  Polly   21
  Sarah   74
  Susan   14

Garton,
  Catharine   46
  Judith   86

George,
  Catharine   95
  Elizabeth   17,53
  Felisha   3
  Frances O.   8
  Jane   36
  Jane M.   47
  Susanna   24,33

Gerauld,
  Elizabeth   35

Gibson,
  Frances   91

Gibson (continued)			Guthery, Guthrie	
Jane	41		Frances	11
Lucy	91		Margret	24
Martha Jane	20			
Virginia Ann	15		**H**	

Gladen,			Hackney,	
Amanda	43		Alice	7
			Catharine	14
Goalman,			Elizabeth	83
Mary	20		Elizabeth L.	83
			Elizabeth M.	50
Good,			Jane	6
Jane	15		Lucy	84
Polly	22		Maria	83
			Priscilla	73
Goode,			Sarah	31
Eleanor	73		Susan H.	61
Elizabeth	18			
Francis	75		Haile,	
			Henrietta	54
Gordon,			Mary	53
Rhoda	80		Sarah	93
Winefred	67			

Green,			Hall,	
Martha	84		Jane	55
Martha J.	64		Lucy	50
Susanna	51		Martha	37
			Sarah	62

Greenwood,			Hanks,	
Elizabeth	34,46		Mary	6
Lucy A.	82			
Nancy	68		Hardin,	
Roenna	29		Lucy	59
Ruth	60		Mary	6
Susan	75			

Groom,			Hardy, Hardee	
Catharine	17		Kitty	77
Martha Ellen	76		Mary	21
			Sarah	89

Grymes,			Harin,	
Alice	64		Rachel	65
Ariana Maria	22			
Jane	72		Harper,	
Mrs. Sarah R.	15		Mary	38
Susanna	15			
			Harrison,	
Gulley,			Mary	35
Charlotte	22			
			Harrow,	
Guthery, Guthrie			Ann	22
Anne	12		Eliza	84

Harrow (continued)		Hodges,	
Lucy	53	Sally	6
Mary F.	66		
Nancy	25	Hodgers,	
		Eleanor	87
Hart,			
Amelia	85	Honsday,	
Mrs. Ann	44	Mary	9
Catherine	21		
Harriet	62	Hord,	
Nancy	17	Emily D.	35
Susannah	18		
		Hoskins,	
Harwood,		Bettie C.	44
Nancy	71	Lucy C. L.	78
Haslewood,		Howard,	
Mary	30	Elizabeth	35,49
		Frances	57
Haynes,		Mary	76
Catharine	78		
Elizabeth	40	Humphries, Humphreys	
		Ann	93
Healy,		Dianah	72
Ann	57	Elizabeth	24
Eliza	67	Elizabeth M.	18
Elizabeth	45	Hannah	52
Elizabeth M.	16,50	Henthia	45
Elizabeth Wood	3	Jane	16
Frances	70	Julia Ann	52
Jane	9	Lucy	71
Juliet M.	30	Lucy E.	78
Maria A.	17	Mary J.	88
M. Augusta	17	Mildred	70
Martha G.	10	Nancy Renn	25
Mary A.	36	Polly	80
Mary E.	11	Susannah S.	61
Polly Clarke	94		
Sarah	81	Hundley, Hunley	
Sarah E.	30	Ann	41
		Elizabeth	9
Hearn,			
Harriett L.	46	Hunt,	
		Betsy	94
Hibble,		Elen	53
Mary	28, 89		
		Hutchings	
Hill,		Mildred	49
Nancy	62		
		J	
Hillyard,			
Mary V.	55	Jackson,	
		Ann	9, 94
		Ann S.	5
Hitchens,		Catharine	1,21,47,79
Ann	26	Charlotte	21

Jackson, continued		Kellom, Kellum	
Elizabeth	37	Jisey	43
Fanny	71	Lucy	43
Frances	46	Mahala	9
Judith	28,55	Mildred	46
Lucinda L.	3	Nancy	24
Martha Ann	67	Polly	25
Mary	4		
Nancy	87	Kemp,	
Sarah	2	Ann	45,60,74
Sarah Ann E.	34	Elizabeth	29
Susannah	5	Hannah	46
Virginia	61	Lucy H.	57

Jacobs,		Kidd,	
Nancy	11,49	Eliza	11
Patty	33	Elizabeth	23,36,65
		Jane	27,48
Jarvis,		Jenny	21
Patsey	72	Judith	87
		Judy	32
Jefferson,		Lucy	74
Grace	5	Maria	87
Mary	94	Martha Ann	25
		Mary Ann	85
Jesse,		Milly	33
Catherine	57	Nancy	48,76,93
Elizabeth	79	Polly	47,73
Frances	26	Ruth	10
Lucy	60	Sally	79

Johnson,		Knight,	
Ann	14	Hannah,	83
Margarett M.	46		

		Knowles	
Jones,		Catharine	2
Catherine	78	Elizabeth	11
Elizabeth	59,89		
Elizabeth M.	39	**L**	
Elizabeth Pope	30		
Fanny	94	Lamkin,	
Frances	90	Elizabeth	27
Frances A.	57		
Judith	96	Lane,	
Lucy	42,71	Elizabeth	29
Margaret	84		
Martha	31	Laughlin,	
Rosa	59	Elizabeth	4
Rosetta	18	Ursula	81
Sarah	56		

K

		Layton,	
Kee, Key		Elizabeth	2,3
Betsy	38	Mary	3,75
Elizabeth	59	Sophia	25
Jinney	70		
Martha	59	Leaco,	
		Nancy	23

Leakes,
    Caty   29

Lee,
    Ann   57
    Ann H.   85
    Catherine   26
    Charlotte   89
    Dorothy   86
    Elizabeth   1,55,62,85
    Frances   30,57,85
    Jane   12,56
    Joannah   34
    Leanna   31
    Louisa   80
    Lucy   47
    Maria   83
    Mary   5
    Penelope   58
    Rachel   27
    Sarah C.   3
    Ursula   81

Lewis,
    Frances   78
    Martha C.   74
    Mary   35
    Nancy P.   71
    Sarah   9

Lilly,
    Betsy   70
    Eliza   70
    Lucy B.   18

Lister,
    Sarah   11,70

Lomax,
    Elizabeth   77

Long,
    Elizabeth   47
    Joanna   7
    Mary   76
    Nora   3
    Sarah   3

Longest,
    Nancy   93

Lorimer,
    Isabella   30

M

Maderris, Maderis, Meaderis
    Ailcy   26
    Ann   16
    Elizabeth   16
    Harriet   42
    Judith   26
    Mary   38,51
    Ophelia   11

Madiex,
    Frances   31

Maggs, Meggs, Meigs
    Christiana   48
    Polly   20
    Rutha   93
    Sally   34

Major,
    Elizabeth   44
    Elizabeth C.   64
    Harriet J.   77
    Louisa M.   60
    Lucy Ann   71
    Martha   51
    Polley M.   78

Marchant,
    Charlotte   71

Marshall,
    Peggy   6

Martin,
    Lucy   16

Mason,
    Elizabeth   62
    Sarah F.   50

Matthews,
    Elizabeth   67
    Lucy   25
    Lucy A.   24
    Mary   56

McKan,
    Catharine   89
    Elizabeth   15
    Francis   89
    Jean   89

McKan (continued)
Julia	37
Lucy	19
Molly	19
Polly	29
Rachel	1
Sarah	16

McTyer, McTyre
Catharine	29
Eunice D.	22
Frances	21
Mary E.	33
Sarah E.	92
Sarah Jane	57

Meacham,
Elizabeth	63,79
Jane	33
Lucy	38
Mary	79,80
Sarah	81

Mears,
Sarah Ann	14

Mercer,
Elizabeth	19
Judith	83
Mary Elizabeth	56

Mickelburrough,Mickelborough
Ann	13
Caty	47
Elizabeth	4,41
Jane	97
Julia	42
Lucy	73
Margaret S.	42
Mary	74
Nancy	34
Nancy Taylor	44

Miles,
Betsey	43
Jane (Jean)	38
Maria	5
Mary Anna	14
Precilla	27
Sarah	44

Miller,
Adeline	4
Ann	50

Miller (continued)
Ann Elizabeth	7
Anna H.	6
Crissy	8
Elizabeth	80
Nancy Davis	75
Nancy G.	7
Polly A.	64
Sarah	76

Mills,
Elizabeth	66

Minter,
Mary	94
Susanna	44

Mitchell,
Sarah	40

Montague, Mountague
Ann	21
Ann Y.	16
Anna Frances	95
Catherine	57,59,63,74
Charlotte	57,59,89
Clarissa	49
Eliza	69
Elizabeth	58
Elizabeth S.	57
Frances	19,40,59
Jane	4,43,86,97
Martha	57
Martha A.	24
Mary Katharine	59
Penelope	73
Sarah S.	30

Montgomery,
Jane	62
Mary C.	93
Salley	38
Susan A.	67

Moore,
Elizabeth	66
Fanny	13
Nancy	42
Sally	78
Susanna	67

Morgan,
Ann	82
Jane	26

Morgan,(continued)

    Joanna   49

    Letitia   40

    Sarah Gale   50

Morris,

    Elizur A.   47

Moulson,

    Judy   28

Mountain,

    Lucy Ann   68

    Mary M.   93

Muire,

    Matilda   25

Mullins,

    Nancy   43

Murray,

    Anne   22

    Caty   69

    Harriot   61

    Lucy   97

    Mary   51

    Sally   69

Muse,

    Betty T. C.   23

    Juliet   20

    Mary S.   36

    Mirenda   31

    Virginia E.   35

N

Neal,

    Sarah E.   8

Neilson, Nielson

    Agnes   60

    Jane   78

New,

    Mary   39

Newcomb,

    Caroline   7

    Elizabeth   87

Nicolson,

    Sarah Tayloe   66

Noel,

    Maria G.   34

    Susan S.   60

Norton,

    Elizabeth   28,62

    Frances   18

O

Oakes,

    Mary Elizabeth   53

Oliver,

    Catharine   32

    Frances   37

    Matilda   3,32

O'Neal,

    Mary E.   90

Owen,

    Ann   81

    Arreanna M.   39

    Betsey   45

    Catherine   79

    Juliett E.   39

    Lucy   65

    Martha   16

    Mary   6

    Molly   53

    Rebecca   87

    Sarah   10,13

P

Pace,

    Elizabeth Elliott   84

    Virginia A.   3

Palmer,

    A.M.F.   81

    Ann E.   52

    Emaline   88

    Judith   3

    Mary A. E.   64

    Matilda J.   69

    Nancy   81

    Sarah C.   95

    Sarah F.   16

Pamplin,

    Mary   5

Parker,

    Frances Ann   50

    Mary   76

Parker (continued)		Poythress,	
Sally	10	Elizabeth	31
Susanna	67		
		Price,	
Parron,		Mary	5
Ann C.	92		
Catharine M.	54	Pritchett,	
Maria	49	Eliza J.	50
Mary E.	54	Elizabeth	2
Nancy	92	Mary A.	38
Parrot, Parrott		Pryor,	
Ann	51,91	Elizabeth	86
Parry,		Purks,	
Catharine A.	65	Frances	90
Lucy P.	26		
		R	
Payne,			
Betty	93	Read,Reade	
		Elizabeth	58
		Frances	43
Peade,		Nancy	7,58
Mary J.	18	Sarah	71
Phillips		Respess,	
Susannah	77	Lucy Ann J.B.	29
Piper,		Reveer, Revere	
Priscilla	14	Ann M.	88
		Anna Catharine	37
Pitts,		Hannah	88
Martha A.	87	Mildred	14
		Sarah C.	68
Plater, Plator		Sarah F.	88
Elizabeth	46		
Rebecca	82	Rhodes,	
		Ann	83
Pool,		Lucy	5
Amanda	64	Sarah	4
Porter,		Rice,	
Kittury	28	Hannah	34
Potter,		Richeson,	
Hannah	82	Elizabeth	84
Powell,		Richardson,	
Lucy Billups	87	Lucy	63
Susan	9	Sarah	10
Powers,		Ridgway,	
Martha A.	21	Henrietta	66
Mary	81		

Rilee
　Mary　20

Risby,
　Lucy　39

Roane,
　Ann F.　77
　Catherine　63
　Cornelia E.　30
　Elizabeth　61
　Frances Daniel　9
　Harriott　39
　Lucy　86
　Lucy Elizabeth B.　95
　Mary　51
　Nancy　73
　Patsey Hipkins　69
　Polly　73

Robinson,
　Ann　90
　Ann E.　82
　Catherine　28
　Eliza　51
　Elizabeth　5,17,79,90,91
　Elvira　45
　Judith　10
　Lucy L.　83
　Nancy　15
　Polley C.　88
　Sally　45
　Sarah　6,36
　Ursala　70
　Willantina　82

Rogers,
　Ann　82

Rose,
　Mary D.　2

Ross,
　Ann　23
　Frances　55

Row,
　Rebecca　4

S

Sadler,
　Feby　24
　Mary　28

St. John,
　Frances　12
　Mary Ann　12

Saunders, Sanders
　Ann　11
　Avarilla　56
　Betty　7
　Chrisse　7
　Crissy　64
　Elizabeth　13,84
　Mary　56,73
　Nancy　11
　Sally　91
　Sally S.　3

Sayre,
　Mary Grymes　10

Scott,
　Nancy　1,40
　Sally　9

Scrosby,
　Anne　48
　Dorothy　14
　Elizabeth　20

Sears,
　Caroline　20
　Jane　37
　Lucy　17
　Nancy　88,96
　Polley　12

Segar,
　Catherine　30
　Jane　60
　Judith　29
　Maria E.　16
　Mary　59
　Priscilla　83

Seward,
　Almira　63
　Ann B.　10
　Catharine　72
　Elizabeth　13,28,33,39
　Elizabeth E.　33
　Leonora　12
　Lucy　12
　Lucy Ann B.　73
　Mary S.　55
　Nancy　35,73

Seward (continued)
Polly T.	29
Rebecca	11
Roberta	1
Susanna	74

Shackelford,
Elizabeth	45

Sharod, Sharrod
Rachel	53
Susan A.	85

Shelton,
Catherine	8
Winney	90

Shepherd,
Caty Price	34
Eunice B.	95
Julia D.	19
Mary	74
Mary E.	96
Mary Elizabeth	95

Shipley,
Isabella	29
Jane	61
Nancy	89

Shurles,
Ann	67

Sibley,
Ann H.	8
Frances D.	88
Harriet	47
Julian D.	7
Lucy	80
Matilda	23
Nancy	28
Susanna	10

Simco,
Martha	91,96

Skelton,
Mary	60

Small,
Mary	77

Smith,
Caroline	48
Elizabeth S.	19

Smith (continued)
Esther	91
Frances	26
Frankey	95
Martha	71
Mary	43,46,83,84
Ruth	4
Sarah	12

Snelling,
Elizabeth	91

Sommers,
Sarah	86

South,
Frances A.	12
Lucy	41
Polly	35
Sara A.	66
Sarah	34

Southall,
Jane	60

Southern,
Avey	73,82

Spann, Span
Elizabeth	50
Jane	50
Juliet	91
Polly	28
Priscilla	2

Spratt,
Charlotte	36

Staige,
Lucia	24

Stamper,
Ann	91
Elizabeth	8,16
Martha G.	39
Sally	48

Stanard,
Elizabeth	97
Ester	87

Stant,
Fama Ann	18

Stapleton,			Taylor (continued)		
Elizabeth	46		Rosa A.	35	
Steptoe,			Terrier,		
Sarah Robinson	36		Sarah	36	
Stevens,			Thacker,		
Mary	24		Anne	89	
Nancey	76		Frances	10	
Priscilla	42		Sarah	40	
Stiff,			Thomas,		
Avarilla	71		Dalinda	32	
Betty	6		Virginia A.	77	
Elizabeth B.	96				
Elizabeth D.	81		Thurston, (Thruston)		
Fanny M.	77		Ann C.	6	
Lucia	89		Catharine	47	
Mary	36,72		Elizabeth	55,90	
Mary C.	90		Frances	49	
Nancy	70		Mary	92	
Sarah W.	23				
			Timberlake,		
Street,			Hannah Thacker	51	
Elizabeth	44				
Frances	58		Todd,		
Lucy Ann	33		Elenor	76	
Susanna	54		Priscilla	82	
Stubblefield,			Towill,		
Elizabeth	2		Mary Elizabeth Ann	44	
Sutton,			Trader,		
Elizabeth	15		Pamela	25	
Lucy	60		Parmelia	85	
Maria	17		Rebecca Ann	25	
Mary	36		Sarah	41	
Michal	37				
Nancy	27		Trice,		
Sarah	29		Betty C.	46	
			Catharine	15	
Swords,			Catharine C.	74	
Catharine	47		Charlotte Ann	54	
Elizabeth	58		Dorothea M.	55	
			Frances	19	
T			Frances J.	74	
			Laura A. F.	55	
Taff,			Martha A.	83	
Mary	1		Mary M.	57	
Nancy	33		Peggy	22	
Priscilla	53		Polly	45	
			Rebecca	50	
Taylor,			Turner,		
Elizabeth	27		Catharine	86	
			Caty	96	

Turner (continued)

Elizabeth	96
Martha	56
Polly	34
Sally	34

V

Valentine,

Elizabeth	58

Vance,

Margaret	33

Vass,

Catharine	57,59
Elizabeth	49
Martha	44

Vaughan,

Arena	67
Elizabeth	38,62
Fanny	62
Martha	44

W

Wake,

Ann	82
Anna Maria	61
Dorothy	28
Elizabeth	48,56
Joanna	95
Lucy	52
Mary	64,89
Mary E.	33

Walden,

Amanda	54
Frances	96
Jane	72
Louisa	54
Nancy	12
Susanna	69

Walker,

Ann F.	77
Betsy Bushrod	25
Clara	1
Cordelia	61
Elenor	55
Emerald	8
Julia J.	88
Mary Elizabeth	30
Sarah	64

Walton,

Penelope	37

Ward,

Mary S.	70

Ware,

Ann J.	85
Caty	45
Catharine	36
Eliza	24
Elizabeth	83,96
Frances	56,67
Jane	13
Nancy	56,62,71
Rebecca	90
Susanna	96

Warwick,

Casandra	54
Jane	34

Washington,

Charlotte	61

Watts,

Alcie	15
Ann	32
Catharine	85
Elizabeth	1,40
Frances	90
Hannah	92
Julia	94
Lucy	32
Lydia	88
Mary M. H.	87
Nancy	72
Parke Harley	68
Sally	94
Sarah	93

Watson,

Mary	12

Weatherspon,

Sally	92

Webb,

Myra	39

Webbmore (Webmore)

Sally	4

Whiting,

Elizabeth H.	17

(18)

Whiting (continued)
Mary Robinson   22

Wilcox,
   Frances   71
   Martha   49

Wilkins,
   Avery   95
   Elizabeth   12,65
   Julia   91
   Lucy   48
Williams,
   Harriett   72
   Jean   38
   Judith   78
   Lucy   48
   Polly   23,90
   Rachel   8
   Sarah   49
Williamson,
   Lucy   63
   Sally   92
   Sarah   14

Wilson,
   Mary   54

Wood,
   Alice   32
   Ann   24
   Elizabeth   70
   Fanny   32
   Frances   4,14
   Hannah U.   39
   Lucy Ann   37
   Mary   32
   Mary Ann   27
   Mary E.   26
   Mary J.   80
   Mary M.   19
   Sarah   8
   Sarah N.   52
   Susanna   80

Woodford
   Fanny   66
   Nancy   26

Woodley,
   Alice   25
   Elizabeth   49
   Nancy   38

Woods,
   Eleanor H.   68

Woodward,
   Ann Frances   69
   Caroline A.   77
   Elizabeth   30
   Elizabeth R. B.   96
   Isabella R.   75
   Lucy   75
   Matilda Ann Eliz^a Temple   53

Wormeley,
   Agatha   68
   Elizabeth   26
   Jane   5
   Judith   36
   Sarah   70

Wortham,
   Ann   21,46,77,80,95
   Anne Catharine   66
   Fanny   90
   Katy   32
   Lucy   77
   Nancy F.   64

Wyatt, Wiatt
   Catey   48
   Elizabeth   42,48
   Frances   2,32
   Frances L.   61
   Lucy F.   4
   Nancy   91,96
   Polly   63
   Susannah   68

Wyett,
   Elizabeth   36

Y

Yarrington,
   Judith   14
   Mary   19

Yates,
   Anne   79
   Catherine   59
   Catharine B.   4
   Elizabeth S.   68
   Rachel Murray Beverley   20
   Sarah   17
Young,
   Parmelia   89

www.ingramcontent.com/pod-product-compliance
Lightning Source LLC
Chambersburg PA
CBHW021834020426
42334CB00014B/624